$3-95
Grr
Y0-EEK-328

A Westland gold prospector in the eighties; the Makawhio (Jacobs) River from a virgin col at the head of the Maitahi valley; an exploring party in the head of the Rangitata in 1934; John Pascoe, Priestley Thomson, Duncan Hall, Gavin Malcolmson.

A missionary party in a swamp

Explorers fording the Taramakau River

EXPLORATION
NEW ZEALAND

John Pascoe

EXPLORA

NEW

A panorama of the Ruahine Range.

DU
411
P318
1971

TION

ZEALAND

A. H. & A. W. REED

A surveyor's drawing from Mount Lord on the Rakaia Divide. The mountains on the left are Whitcombe, and Roberts; those on the skyline are Louper, Butler and Ramsay.

LIBRARY
ST. LOUIS
ART MUSEUM

DU
411
P318
1971

First published 1971

A. H. & A. W. REED LTD.
182 Wakefield Street, Wellington
29 Dacre Street, Auckland
165 Cashel Street, Christchurch
51 Whiting Street, Artarmon, Sydney
357 Little Collins Street, Melbourne

© 1971   John Dobrée Pascoe

ISBN 0 589 00667 3

This book is copyright. Except for purposes of
private study, criticism or review, no part may be
reproduced by any process including stencilling or
photocopying without the prior written permission
of the publishers.

Set by Commercial Print Ltd., Wellington.
Printed by Dai Nippon Printing Co. (International) Ltd.,
Hong Kong.

A beech forest in Wellington.

29375

*for Anna and Ian Gilmour
and their family*

A flooded branch of the Arawhata River, Westland.

Acknowledgments and Sources

I wrote this book from the accounts of New Zealand explorers and in light of my own knowledge of some of the country described by their editors or biographers. I have illustrated the text with sketches, drawings, engravings, paintings and photographs using the historical and contemporary material from the sources here acknowledged. For a select reading list I recommend the various missionary papers and local and regional histories which should be studied against the background of W. G. McClymont's *The Exploration of New Zealand* (Wellington, 1940) and some of my own writings and those of Herries Beattie of Waimate about exploration.

I am grateful to many people for generous help: A. G. Bagnall, Miss Muriel Lord, and Mrs Janet Blackwood Paul of the Alexander Turnbull Library; Miss J. S. Hornabrook and staff of the National Archives; S. R. Strachan of the Hocken Library; the Rev L. R. M. Gilmore of Morrinsville and Miss R. S. McKay of Gisborne; Dr P. B. Maling who put me on to the Heaphy sketches in the British Museum. Messrs Whitcombe and Tombs Ltd. have allowed me to use the Lauper map and the Pegasus Press to reproduce E. Mervyn Taylor's drawing on page 94. The authors and/or publishers of the following books have kindly allowed me to quote from their pages: A. H. & A. W. Reed, *The Letters and Journals of Samuel Marsden*, ed. by J. R. Elder (Dunedin, 1932); *William Colenso . . .* by A. G. Bagnall and G. C. Petersen (Wellington, 1948); Collins-Cheshire, *The Hero as Murderer* by Geoffrey Dutton (London, 1967); Simpson & Williams, *Pioneers on Port Cooper Plains* by John Deans (Christchurch, 1964); Oxford University Press, *Early Travellers in New Zealand* by Nancy M. Taylor (Oxford, 1959).

I thank these people and institutions for allowing me to use the illustrations as follows: Alexander Turnbull Library: end paper (*left*), pages 1, 11, 12, 13, 16, 19, 20, 21, 27, 30, 31, 32 (*bottom*), 34 (*left*), 35, 37, 40, 54 (*bottom*), 55, 58, 59, 65 (*bottom*), 75, 77, 78 (*top*), 81 (*bottom*), 92, 98, 100, 101, 104, 105 (*bottom left*), 106, 107, 108, 111, 115, 116, 118, 127, 128 (*bottom*), 129, 131 (*bottom*), 135 (*top*), 137; colour pages 1, 2, 4, 7, and dust jacket. Many of these illustrations came from *Making New Zealand,* a Government Centennial publication of 1940 of which I was the illustrations editor. Auckland City Art Gallery, page 8; colour page 5; H. Andrews, page 91 (*bottom*); Auckland Institute & Museum, page 47; H. McD. Baker, page 67; Cranleigh Barton, page 30 (*right*); V. C. Browne, page 136 (*top*); K. & J. Bigwood, page 46; British Museum, pages 61, 62; Anita Crozier, page 138 (*right*); A. P. Druce, pages 2, 28, 45 (*right*); Ian Deans pages 95, 96; *Dunedin Punch*, page 135 (*top*); I. A. Gilmour (*inside dust jacket*); Peter Graham, 110 (*bottom*); F. G. Hall-Jones, pages 120, 123; Hawke's Bay Art Gallery and Museum, pages 44, 45 (*left*); Hocken Library, pages 37, 128, 135; D. Matheson page 138 (*left*); J. H. Johns, New Zealand Forest Service, pages 71, 74; Mitchell Library, Sydney, pages 18, 32; National Archives, colour pages 3, 8; National Art Gallery, page 111, colour page 6; Nelson Historical Society (Tyree collection) pages 54 (*top*), 57; National Library of Australia (Rex Nan Kivell collection), page 34 (*right*); Ted Porter, page 88 (*bottom*); *Punch in Canterbury*, page 97 (*top*); R.N.Z.A.F., P. L. D. Cummins, page 109 (*bottom*); P. G. Webster, page 25; Tourist & Publicity Dept., pages 10, 17, 23, 26, 65 (*top*), 119 (*top*), 131 (*top*). For the record, my own photographs are: pages 4, 5, 7, 29, 38, 41, 42, 50, 52, 56, 63, 66, 69, 70, 72, 73, 78 (*bottom*), 79, 81 (*top*), 83, 84, 85, 86, 87, 88 (*top*), 89, 91 (*top*), 94 (*bottom*), 97 (*bottom*), 105 (*right*), 109 (*top*), 110 (*top*), 113, 114, 119 (*bottom*), 125, 132, 133, 134.

The cover block (gold leaf) was drawn by Sara Tun. The maps were reproduced by permission of the Department of Lands and Survey and were drawn by W. G. Harding, pages 14, 27, 57, 80, 82, 86, 95, 106, 112, 117, 122, 134; C. Holdsworth, page 90; Julius Petro, pages 24, 39, 44, 69, 121, 126, back end paper. Neville Atkinson did the colour photography. I did the layout of the illustrations and F. A. Davey, the typography.

Contents

A storm cloud forms on Mount Aspiring above the Matukituki valley.

C. F. Goldie painted gaunt men making landfall.

K. Watkins imagined the scene to be tranquil.

Two versions of the arrival of the Maoris in New Zealand.

Introduction

No place in New Zealand is a great distance from the sea. Many places have names of Maori origin. These facts are vivid reminders that our land forms are young, and that our period of human occupation is not ancient in the sense that old countries and old civilisations understand and are sustained by antiquity.

The sequence of geological history in New Zealand lies through millions of years from the oldest fossils to the current evidence of volcanic activity or glacier retreat. The sequence of New Zealand's human history includes many hundreds of years of Polynesian settlement; we can greatly regret our scant knowledge of Maori exploration. It is certain that Maori trails formed a network in the North Island, where the abundance of eels in the rivers and lakes and of birds, roots and berries in the bush made travel feasible. Maori trails in the South Island were blocked in many places by high and snowy mountains. The absence of written records for the daring Maori navigators who located New Zealand in the vast Pacific or were blown off course to its island welcome is not a negation of history. The proud genealogies of the Maori settlers and their forerunners emphasise their capacity to record their origins in their own way. The further research material now available to archaeologists may yet unravel some of the puzzling threads of the tangled skeins of tribal history.

Tribal conflict as well as tribal cohesion accounted for some of the journeys of Maori exploration. When the first European settlers arrived they had it made, so to speak, so far as many of the routes to the interior of the North Island were concerned. All that they needed were Maori guides.

It was different in the South Island where good harbours were few and where some of the best harbours, as in the country now known as Fiordland, were landlocked by precipices. The Maori population of the South Island was not much more than a total of 3 per cent of the whole Maori population. There was more wild country in the South and more to be explored. There were Maori guides, but not in the numbers of the North Island, and none could be said to be trained, whether by tradition or in practice, in the difficulties of mountain travel which would inevitably be thrust on future explorers.

Significant dates of Maori exploration in either island must be as misty as the legends from which they sprang. Significant dates in European exploration can be more precise. Nobody today doubts that 1642 was the year of the earliest European contact with New Zealand or that it was made by the great Dutch navigator Abel Janszoon Tasman. There have been theories that an earlier landfall was made by a Frenchman, a Spaniard or a Portuguese but the most careful examination by an historian and geographer of the evidence cannot support such claims. With Tasman as the beginning of our European knowledge of New Zealand we must credit his great successor Captain James Cook with coastline charting, with both an understanding of the Maoris and an observation of the natural features of their land. As Cook's leading biographer, J. C. Beaglehole, observed: "There had never been discovery like this before."

The diversity of the country was to be both attraction and challenge. Climate, soil, rocks, forest, rivers, islands: there were differences even in a hundred miles. Even in this age of reliable road, rail and air transport it is possible for floods and storms to disrupt journeys. Cast your mind to the time when there were no maps or knowledge of the interior. Consider that the rivers were unbridged and their sources uncertain. Imagine that no one knew what lay over the other side of the hills on your horizon. Only then can you feel some of the doubts that must have assailed travellers on some of the first major journeys. What was needed to overcome such doubts? Curiosity; evangelism; the search for gold or for grazing; adventure; restlessness; energy: any combination of these could be ingredients for enterprise and hazard.

I have felt some of these doubts for myself. My on-and-off mountaineering career of some forty-one years has included occasional forays into country not well known or well mapped.

My editing and biographical work on explorers such as Thomas Brunner, Sir James Hector, Charles Douglas and Jakob Lauper has taken me sometimes over some of their trails, even into their states of mind, to the point that I have dreamt that I have had glimpses of their company. To attempt a lucid and concise illustrated text of exploration in New Zealand I have divided each main island into three regions. Each region has its own time sequence. Inevitably some regions will interlock or overlap. A really energetic missionary could and did walk over more than one region on a single expedition. Good transalpine trips could include two regions. Yet some arbitrary divisions had to be devised, else the text could squelch into a puzzling morass of place-names under a fog of dates.

9

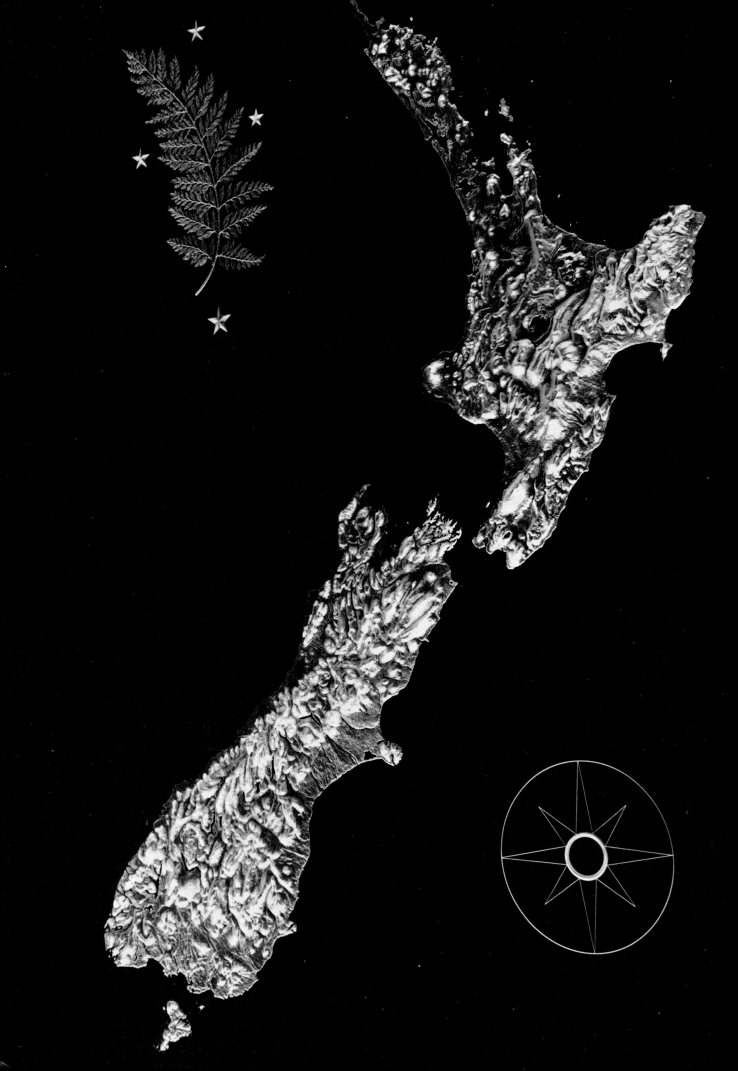

Northland to the East Cape and Coast

Here I can compare the cradle of history with home terrain of Maori warriors, the birth of storms with the death of forest, the precursors of trade with the hang-over of evangelism. The salt of the sea and the mud of the mangrove inlet, the torrid force of rivers, the composure of swamps and the stately boles of the kauri are elements in keeping with a mild climate and a varied coastline. A scatteration of islands herald the eastern dawn; the uncompromising surge of rollers from the Tasman Sea holds steady from the west.

The accuracy of the coastline chart of 1770 of the North Island by Lieutenant J. Cook, Commander of His Majesty's *Endeavour,* contrasts with the repetitive hillocks of the interior. The first book written about New Zealand after Cook was by John Savage, who visited the Bay of Islands in 1805 as surgeon of a convict ship. His three plates show respectively the head of a Maori chief, a *tiki,* and a coastal scene. For the first exploration beyond the coastline, and an account of such travel, the source is the missionary: in particular, one missionary, Samuel Marsden.

James Cook and Samuel Marsden had the same part of England as origin: Yorkshire; the same virtues so necessary to their adventures: self-discipline and courage. Like Cook's, Marsden's origin was humble. As convict's chaplain in New South Wales from 1794 Marsden showed some versatility: magis-trate, farmer and priest. His reputation in Australian history is one of failure as evangelist, but no biography of him in depth has yet been written. His reputation in New Zealand is kinder. The editor of his journals wrote of the abiding admiration Marsden gained from Maori warriors who regarded his courage as the essential virtue in man. An Australian writer, A. T. Yarwood, recently summed up Marsden's "substantial achievement in New Zealand . . . he was a sincere and devoted Christian evangelist with a robust faith in his mission to proclaim the gospel and save souls. Marsden's efforts made possible a tangible and impressive victory, as measured in his lifetime by the imparting of British techniques and values, by the suppression of cannibalism, the growth of literacy, and the eventual scale of conversion and church membership."

Coastal scenes in 1805 as shown by John Savage.

The landing of Samuel Marsden on Christmas Day, 1814, as recorded by a missionary publication.

Marsden certainly had faith. The first night that he slept on New Zealand soil he wrote: "The night was clear, the stars shone brightly, and the sea in our front was smooth. Around us were numerous spears stuck upright in the ground and groups of natives lying in all directions like a flock of sheep upon the grass, as there were neither tents nor huts to cover them." That same night, 19 December 1814, was also described by J. L. Nicholas, a New South Wales landowner who accompanied Marsden: "The ground was our bed, and we had no other covering than the clothes we wore . . . I slept tolerably well for some part of the night, and awaking at the dawn of day, a scene, the strangest that can be imagined, presented itself to my view. An immense number of human beings, men, women and children, some half naked, and others loaded with fantastic finery, were all stretched about me in every direction."

On Christmas Day Marsden began his service with the Old Hundredth Psalm, and continued with his sermon of the "glad tidings of great joy". His journeys inland on this first visit were short. Nicholas described the country towards Waimate as "gentle eminences, covered in some places with fern". A walk to Hongi's pa was varied by canoe travel. The obstacles of New Zealand bush became apparent: "We experienced the same annoyance in our progress through this wood, as we did in the forest at Wycaddee [Waikare], the underwood being equally troublesome, crossing and intersecting the path in every direction; besides

we had to get over a stream running in the middle of it, which was attended with some difficulty." At Lake Omapere the party reached its farthest west.

Marsden made some short visits from his brig *Active* and left Thomas Kendall and John King behind at the Bay of Islands station. In June 1819 these men crossed the island to the mouth of the Hokianga river, a trip soon to be repeated by Marsden with three other missionaries. He made his most significant travel in 1820, when one of two warships seeking kauri spars had brought him to New Zealand as a passenger. He went ashore in the Bay of Islands and the Thames. He was later disappointed in his hopes of exploring the Waikato: "The natives who had come as my guides from Wyekotto [Waikato] informed me I could not return with them, because I should not be able to pass the rivers and creeks on the road — they would be too deep for me to ford."

Although he had arranged to travel north by canoe some delay with the Maoris made him impatient: "I now resolved to walk to the Bay of Islands. . . All the chiefs told me I could not make my way to the Bay of Islands on the east side of New Zealand, as the sea-shore in many places was nothing but high rocks which I could not pass. Neither could I cross the rivers nor head the bays which ran into the sea on the east side. If I was determined to go, I must take my route by Kiperro [Kaipara] on the west side and strike off into the interior of the country in order to head the main rivers or bays."

12

His guide talked of swamps. As to rivers, the Maoris told Marsden "they would carry me across the river in a hammock, as they carried the wounded from the field of battle."

On 17 August 1820 Marsden's party left the head of the Waitemata Harbour. The *Journal* is well written; it passes from wet clothes to dry clothes, details of Maori customs and Marsden's evangelism, the vitality of the children, the loads of potatoes and pork, the old tracks through the kauri forests, the interludes in canoes, the hazards and the discomfort. "I was conducted up the narrow pass which I could not ascend without assistance," Marsden wrote, "the path was so steep and narrow." The pa at the head of the track had people and food; snapper, crayfish

Samuel Marsden in 1808

and fern-root. He added: "It was now quite dark. The roaring of the sea at the foot of the hippah [pa], as the waves rolled into the deep caverns beneath, the high precipice upon which we stood, whose top and sides were covered with huts, and the groups of natives conversing round their fires, all tended to excite new and strange ideas for reflection."

His age of fifty-five years must have told against him: "We found the road very bad as it lies along the sea-coast. We had continually to strike off into the woods in order to cross the high necks of land which run out into the sea, and then to descend again to the beach. Several swamps and runs of water we met with on our road through which we had to wade."

The characteristic contrast between canoe travel and cliff hanging, so to speak, must have been hard for a man unused to continuous physical exertions. But he found his experiences rewarding in one sense: "I now felt myself very happy in having got within one short day's journey of the Bay of Islands after an absence of three months . . . nor had I suffered any material injury from cold and wet and want of my proper rest, though I had lain down in my clothes for the last three weeks in boisterous weather in whatever situation the night overtook me."

When he reached Whangaruru and later Pairoa in the Bay of Islands he found the food, the conversation and the rest all sweet on the whaler *Catherine*: "I put a much greater estimate on the blessings I had always enjoyed in civil and religious society than I had ever done before." News from his family and friends was more than welcome.

After a rest at Keri Keri, Marsden left in a whale-boat with two companions, passed Cape Brett (scene of today's tourists' deep-sea fishing) and camped on a beach. Tribal warfare made it inadvisable for Marsden to make an overland journey to the Kaipara. He continued to run the gauntlet of sea, breezes, narrow passages, surf and shelter. By 9 November they had walked from Panmure (to use modern names) through Epsom and so to the Manukau.

It is difficult to think of Auckland, now the city of half a million people and countless local bodies, of political might and industrial wealth, as the site of a city where the only Pakehas were these missionaries, where the route from Onehunga to Ponsonby lay on a trail over the top of Mount Albert, and where progress up the Waitemata depended on tide and the mending of a leaky canoe. Marsden and his party headed for the West Coast near Muriwai, where Maoris sought in solitude a refuge from the wars.

On 13 November the day's journey was exceptionally tiring. One of Marsden's companions wrote: "We walked on the sea beach upwards of twenty miles,

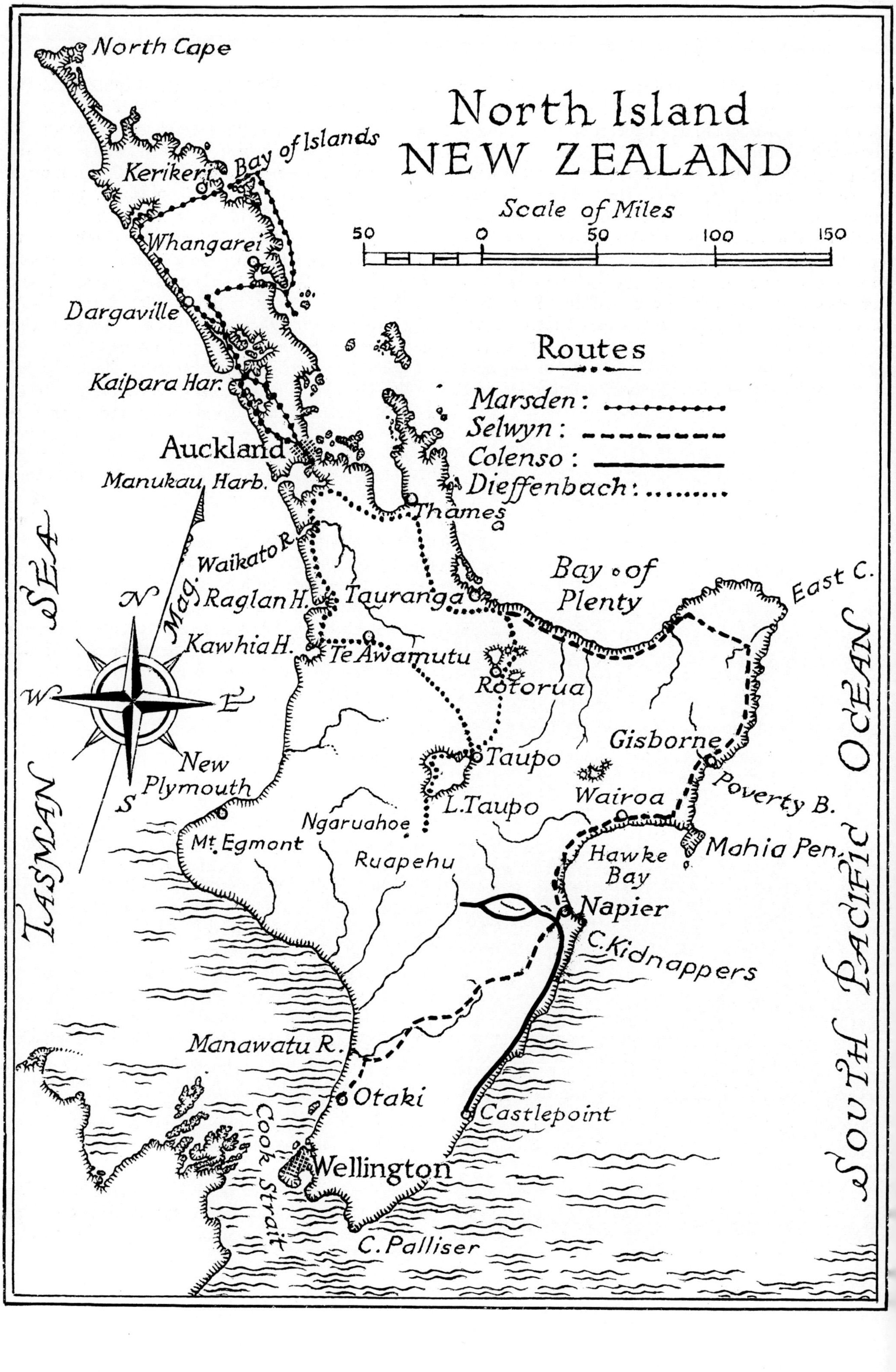

North Cape

Kerikeri
Bay of Islands

Whangarei

Dargaville

Kaipara Har.

Auckland
Manukau Harb.

Waikato R.

Raglan H.
Tauranga
Te Awamutu
Kawhia H.

Rotorua

New
Plymouth

Taupo
L. Taupo

Wairoa

Ngaruahoe

Mt. Egmont

Ruapehu

Hawke
Bay

Napier
C. Kidnappers

Manawatu R.

Otaki
Castlepoint

Wellington

C. Palliser

SEA
TASMAN
Mag. N

North Island
NEW ZEALAND

Scale of Miles

50   0   50   100   150

Routes

Marsden: ....
Selwyn: -----------
Colenso: _____
Dieffenbach: ....

Thames

Bay of
Plenty

East C.

Gisborne
Poverty B.
Mahia Pen.

South Pacific Ocean

Cook Strait

this was a very fatiguing march on the sands; and also, we suffered a great deal from thirst as the day was hot and windy and no water to be had for sixteen miles." Some of the sandhills were up to four hundred feet high.

Four days later the party divided; Marsden and another headed north while the others returned to Panmure for the whaleboat.

Marsden varied walking with canoeing. But did not like the heights and the cliffs. At the Maunganui Bluff he wrote: "In some places the rock is perpendicular next the sea, and from its height makes every nerve tremble to look down. The native path is here and there near the edge. I was not able to walk in some parts, but crept along on my hands and knees." The awe of the scenery would have been little less than the awe of its history; there had been a great battle at this bluff.

Marsden's guides were careful to avoid another Maori party they had glimpsed, and at Hokianga he learnt details of the southern raid and heard the wailing of the women who had lost husbands and warriors. A canoe took him up the Hokianga Harbour. The next day they followed bush trails with this difference: they had no Maori guides. Later they met the chief Patuone whose son guided them towards Whangaroa: "Our road lay in the thick woods nearly the whole way. We had to pass through deep ravines and over very high hills, which made the journey extremely fatiguing."

At last Marsden boarded the *Dromedary*. His final account from his Journal was succinct: "I had been absent from the ship five weeks and one day, during which period I travelled by land and water, about six hundred miles by estimation, and in some of the worst roads that can be conceived. This must naturally be expected, as the country in this respect is in its aboriginal state — no swamps drained, no bridges over rivers or creeks, no rubbish cleared from the paths. A New Zealander finds no difficulty crossing the deep marshes, swamps or deep rivers. Through the one he wades and through the other he swims at his ease."

If Marsden was placing in perspective the Maori skills of bush navigation and river crossing his admirers have similarly paid him a just tribute: "There is something awesome about this man, trudging on foot through hundreds of miles of wild country, bearding the Maori chiefs on their own ground, giving them hoes and seeds intermixed with wiggings on having more than one wife, and exhorting them to give up their petty vengeful gods."

Marsden's subsequent journeys in New Zealand till 1837 were visits rather than marathon walks; his exploits in Australia have made him a puzzle to historians: the pious evangelist in him had warred with the vengeful magistrate. Perhaps his New Zealand career is less puzzling and he can be appreciated without adulation or suspicion. The country that he was the first European to traverse has changed. The remnants of giant forest give way to motorways and orchards. Even the coastal headlands where Marsden shivered with a horror of heights have become insignificant as seen by passing aircraft and are barely visible from deep-sea fishing launches.

As with other parts of New Zealand, Northland was sometimes well described by artists using their pens as well as their drawing materials. In the late 1820s Augustus Earle made valuable records. His *Distant View of the Bay of Islands* is a fine painting, but his *Native Village and Cowdie Forest* is overstylised, to the point that this representation of Patuone's habitat forty miles up the Hokianga river should be considered in conjunction with this text: "We landed in a dense forest, which reached to the water's edge; and our guides and slaves began to divide the loads each was to carry on his back . . . . When our natives had distributed the luggage, they loaded themselves, which they did with both skill and quickness; for a New Zealander is never at a loss for cords or ropes. Their plan is to gather a few handfuls of flax, which they soon twist into a very good substitute: with this material they formed slings, which they dexterously fastened our moveables on their backs, and set off at a good trot, calling out to us to follow them.

"We travelled through a wood so thick that the light of heaven could not penetrate the trees that composed it. They were so large, and so close together, that in many places we had some difficulty to squeeze through them. To add to our perplexities, innumerable streams intersected this forest, which always brought us Europeans to a complete standstill . . . . several times they seated one of us on the top of their load, and carried him over [bridges]."

And now comes Earle's description of the Maori village and kauri forest: ". . . situated on the side of a small picturesque stream, one of the branches of the E.O.Ke Anga [Hokianga] . . . . The red glare of the setting sun, just touching the top of every object, beautifully illuminated the landscape". . .

"The roots of trees covered the path in all directions, rendering it necessary to watch every step we took, in order to prevent being thrown down; the supple jacks, suspended and twining from every tree, making in many places a complete net-work; and while we were toiling with the greatest difficulty through this miserable road our natives were jogging on as comfortably as possible: use had so completely accustomed them to it, that they sprung over the roots, and dived under the supple jacks and branches, with perfect ease, while we were panting after them in vain. The whole way was mountainous. The climbing up, and then descending, was truly frightful."

The over-stylised *Native Village and Cowdie Forest* of Augustus Earle up the Hokianga River.

This insistence on the Maori capacity for guiding and the Pakeha incapacity for the hills that to him were mountainous is a feature of the explorers' narratives of the period.

Traders in the early 1830s took their place with the missionaries in the annals of exploration of the north. Charles Marshall at the age of twenty-two arrived at the Waikato Heads in 1830. He found that Pakehas had considerable mana as atuas (gods). He travelled up the Waikato in a canoe as far as Waipa. Seeing good prospects in trading, he returned to Sydney and then came back to a station he made at the Waikato Heads. A Ngapuhi raid on the Waikato in 1832 destroyed his little empire: "Driven from the Coast, I suffered the extreme of destitution; and but for the kindness of the Natives, whose flight I accompanied, I must have perished." He remained in the interior for four years. This must have been frustrating for him because his earlier travels had taken him on a canoe trip to Otahuhu and the Thames. By 1835 he was making bricks for the Church Mission Society. He married in the following year and his subsequent career lay in the Waikato as a settler.

Another trader who explored by canoe was Philip Tapsell who reached Rotorua from the Bay of Plenty in 1831. But the missionaries again took the stage and it was back again to the north. The Rev. William

16

Williams with several other missionaries and thirty-six Maoris left Whangaroa late in November 1832, the Maoris carrying loads of provisions to last three weeks: "The road being now unfrequented, is quite tedious to pass over, on account of the brushwood." The Maoris travelled slowly; no doubt their burdens were shockers.

Williams was quite explicit about some of the obstacles: "We made a course for the western coast, but over such a road as I have never yet travelled: it lay through a continued swamp, for some miles."

Motorists of today know the beauty of the Mangamuka Gorge road from the Hokianga to Kaitaia. Williams too admired the scenery: "Our tent is now pitched in a most romantic situation, in the midst of a forest, at the conflux of two large rivulets, whose purling streams are beautifully shaded by an endless variety of trees; whilst the indistinct light of the moon, shining through the dense shade, greatly heighten the picture."

This writing was a bit of saccharine, and a trader in 1833 did better with abuse of swamps or mountains:

J. S. Polack wrote: "We passed on our way ascending other hills, on the summits of which we could only see an interminable succession of hills and mountains, rising above each other, separated by fertile valleys, and clothed in the evergreen verdure of this beautiful land." And again: "We found the ascent to the mountains very difficult and tedious; the valleys below were becoming swamps from the heavy torrents that were falling."

If there is anything that annoyed some of the early travellers more than thick bush it was the lack of it. Here is another account from this early period: "It is impossible to imagine anything more dreary or inhospitable than this side of the island. The coast is lined with a series of sandhills, which seem to run inland to a considerable distance; nor is there for miles a tree or a spot of verdure to diversify the sameness of the scene." Another writer was similarly moved: "It has many, many times been grief to mind to see thousands of acres of land lying waste and miles of country desolate and entirely uninhabited."

The Anglican missionaries of the 1830s included the famous Henry Williams, brother of William

The Mangamuka valley between the Hokianga and Kaitaia.

Swamps were among the natural obstacles to explorers in the North Island. This crayon drawing by C. Clarke shows Sir George Grey's party at Matamata.

Williams, A. N. Brown and J. Hamlin, but the Wesleyans J. Whiteley and James Buller were also men of great faith and enterprise. The journeys concentrated in the areas of the Thames and the Waikato as well as the occasional foray in the Auckland-Kaipara-Bay of Islands region. Swamps abounded in the Waikato and the Thames as well as in Northland. Henry Williams's biographer refers to a route ". . . through many swamps, the last one being very deep, but Mr Williams was carried over comfortably with the aid of two poles. Occasionally the bearers were in mud up to their chests."

Henry Williams made his objective clear: ". . . to form at once, with permission of the [Church Mission] Society, a new station at the River Thames; a place at once so eligible in itself; the Natives so numerous; the navigation so easy up the Thames, leading as far as Waikato, the heart of New Zealand; with not only the willingness, but the entreaties, of the Natives to have Missionaries among them."

The missionaries A. N. Brown and J. Hamlin made a long trip from Waimate North to the Thames in 1834. As the *Missionary Register* put it: "It having been considered desirable that the Rev. A. N. Brown and Mr Hamlin should proceed from Paihia, to explore the District of the Waikato, in subserviency to the object of forming Missionary Stations, they proceeded, together with some of the Native Youths attached to them, overland, on this difficult expedition. . .

"Setting forth from Waimate, they proceeded by the Wairo [Wairoa] River, passing Mangakahia and Aotahi, to Kaipara Harbour. Landing here, they travelled by compass through the broken and trackless country in the direction of Waikato; often making their own way, with great difficulty, through fern and bushes. A journey of between 70 and 80 miles, and which occupied seven or eight days, brought them to the Waikato River."

After ten days further travel, the missionaries and

A missionary and his entourage in the 1820's as drawn by De Sainson, a French artist with Dumont d'Urville's expedition.

their guides made rafts of raupo rushes: "On ten of these rudely-shaped floats they paddled across; and found them to answer so well, that they proceeded some miles in them, on the river . . . From a hill in the Waikato Country the Missionaries had a distant view into the centre of the southern part of this island." Mr Brown was quoted: "Ascended Kaka-puku with Mr Hamlin; from whence we saw Tongariro, bearing S.E. by S. about seventy miles off: our guide informed us that there are Natives living in the neighbourhood of that mountain, which has a crater still burning: the sides are covered with white ashes, and there are hot springs at its base. We We also saw Ruapaka [Ruapehu], bearing S.S.E. This immense mountain is covered with snow. . . [It] is visible from Cook's Straits." There seems some confusion here. Ruapehu would certainly have been clear from their Waikato vantage point but not from Cook Strait. From Terawhiti trig station or any point in the Strait west of Makara, Mount Egmont would

be seen on a day when there was no haze nor cloud.

W. Williams, Brown and Morgan made a second trip in the Waikato later in 1834 and were away for four months and three days. They reached Ngarua-wahia. Perhaps one of the most emphatic impressions of these inland tours was the knowledge that each Maori tribe dreaded each other's raids; another was the memory of the discomfort and bad weather: "Mr Williams's feet were very chafed owing to his shoes being too large, and passing many times through water. Walking in the natives' very narrow tracks was awkward . . . In heavy rain, which pelted down for five continuous days, the weary party dragged its way over hill and swamp in this pilgrimage."

The attitude of travellers and settlers to New Zealand bush must have congealed at this period, and was not to become more tolerant for generations later: "I can never efface from my memory my feel-ings of admiration on my first entrance into a New

Zealand forest," wrote one traveller. But the admiration modulated into fear: "It was on a bright sunny day, but the thick luxuriant foliage completely shut out the dazzling rays of the sun, and it was so dark, that although I had two natives with me, I was afraid to venture in very far." Many years later, when New Zealand travellers had come to terms with the bush, appreciating its shelter and its firewood, and being able to find their way with a newly-developed instinct for topographical knowledge, the feeling of fear had changed to one of security.

The Wesleyans of the period were active in Northland and further south. John Whiteley, born in 1806, came to London at the age of twenty-five as a candidate for missionary training he had £6 3s in one pocket, and bread and cheese in the other. His arrival in New Zealand had the usual human overtones of domesticity: "Give one thought to the weary bush-track journey to the Hokianga. Delicate Mary Whiteley, due within 6 weeks to have her first babe, travelled in an arm-chair lashed to manuka poles, and borne shoulder high by Maori lads." Whiteley left his mark in the Waikato region. One of his church historians, William W. H. Greenslade, wrote in a biographical pamphlet: "Canoeing up unexplored rivers; riding his horse up mountain bush tracks, and out in the open wilderness; sleeping, labouring, suffering and worshipping with his new friends, this young Englishman came to love and to be loved by the Waikatos."

His long trip from Kaipara to Wellington with his fellow-Wesleyan James Buller began in November 1839 when they sailed across the Kaipara in Buller's boat. They walked to the Waitemata, across the future site of Auckland, and enjoyed a canoe trip across the mouth of the Manukau and halfway down the Waiuku Peninsula. At the Waikato heads they were the guests of Anglicans: "A long walk along the coast followed, sometimes on the beaches, sometimes over the alternating ridges and valleys inland, until they reached James Wallis's station at Raglan. Buller stayed there several days before crossing to the Aotea Harbour where he yielded to the Maoris' request to stay overnight. Reaching Whiteley's station at Kawhia, Buller had to wait twelve days before securing guides willing to take him south-east into hostile territory."[1]

The subsequent exploration of the region between the North and the East Capes depended on good surveys and mapping. The value of the kauri timber declined as its resources were exploited; the kauri gum industry likewise worked itself out. The transition to other bases of living had sporadic glimpses of the spectacular, such as the discovery of gold in the Coromandel at the Kapanga stream in 1852. Mainly the development of the whole region was linked with the growth of dairying. Places like Albertland at the head of the Kaipara Harbour were chosen as special settlements and its scouts no doubt considered themselves as explorers. They could more correctly be described as a survey party or road-makers.

Today Auckland is firmly established as New Zealand's largest city and most influential political centre; its influence will in turn affect the future of the Northland and Bay of Plenty Country. It is a far cry from the sight of Marsden at the end of an expedition ". . . clothed in rags, covered with mud and red ochre from his near contact with the natives . . . and with an old dirty night-cap on his head."

The country over which his Maori guides led him is now mapped in detail and can be related to precise aerial photographs.

[1] A description of this journey will be continued in a following section.

The mission station at Pepepe, near Taupiri, on the Waikato River, where the artist G. F. Angas was received hospitably.

The Centre of the North Island

Leave the North and the East for the interior. Consider lakes and thermal regions, rivers and forests, scientists as well as missionaries, officials as well as surveyors: consider always the Maori inhabitants who knew the land before the pakeha, who fed him and guided him. Consider Maori villages, pumice-lands as yet unbroken for pastures, bird life as yet unsavaged, inland waters as yet unstocked with trout. Consider a maze of ranges and ridges, valleys and watersheds as yet unmarked by roads or power pylons, railways tracks or hoardings.

Some of the goldminers in the South Island left no record of their travels; there were also adventurous men in the North Island whose fate and experiences are described merely by implication and not by primary evidence. One such man was Andrew Powers, described by W. G. McClymont, a leading historian, as a Scandinavian who went under compulsion from Wanganui to the Bay of Plenty. He had been trading in Maori heads when Taupo Maoris captured him and took him to Rotorua in 1831. Henry Williams, the missionary, sailed to Maketu, Rotorua's port, where P. Tapsell, flax trader, was hospitable. Williams and another missionary visited Rotorua, but his records of the trip were more concerned with the evils of mixed bathing than with a good description of the Maori hosts. Tapsell had probably preceded the missionaries as an explorer of the Rotorua region. Other traders were on the East Coast near Gisborne and at Ngaruawahia in the Waikato.

For a time the Maori tribes were peaceful but in the middle 1830s tribal warfare in the Bay of Plenty-Rotorua region broke out. It was greatly to the credit of the missionaries that many of them remained at their posts and used their powers, as best they could, for peace.

By 1839 the decade of the long walks was on. A missionary periodical of the time referred to the "pioneer journey of the Rev. H. Williams from Wanganui to Tauranga, by way of Taupo and Rotorua". A week's march from Taupo Williams recorded that the Maoris ". . . were very much delighted, I being the first European who had visited them". For much of the time the journal entries are characteristically concerned with matters evangelical, but now and again a description of the country breaks through: "At peep of day we were on the move; climbing over very large trees, and going through low swampy ground [in the Wanganui watershed]. At eight o'clock we were thankful to find ourselves clear of the wood, and entering a level country. The volcano Tongoriro rose before us, the summit covered with snow — a splendid sight! The road we had just concluded was certainly the worst I ever passed over. In many places we had to creep under trees, and again to climb over and walk along the trunks of those which had been blown down . . . We brought up for the night at the foot of Ruapaka [Ruapehu]: the land very high, and apparently but a few feet below the snow which lay on the mountain." On 29 December 1839 Williams and his party arrived at

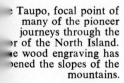

Taupo, focal point of many of the pioneer journeys through the or of the North Island. e wood engraving has ened the slopes of the mountains.

Lake Taupo. Thence they went to Rotorua and Tauranga.

Earlier that year John Carne Bidwill, Australian merchant and amateur botanist, had travelled from Tauranga to Rotorua in the opposite direction. His book *Rambles in New Zealand* has the authentic flavour of the period. He wrote: "I had determined, if possible, to penetrate to those high mountains in the interior of the north island which are shadowed forth on the maps." He had the usual entourage of porters to carry the party gear and provisions. Still, he sensed the feeling of freedom and independence: "There is something inexpressibly delightful in living in a tent: snail-like, you carry your house wherever you go, and for my part, I always sleep much better in a tent than in an inn, sitting at the mouth of my tent like the shepherds of old, than I should if I had the best dinner that ever was cooked in a smoky hotel in London. I recollect while in England that a very little thing would put me out of conceit with my tea . . . but here I always used to think the tea excellent, although boiled in a common tin pot, or pannikan as the sailors call it, and drunk out of the same, and sweetened with coarse brown sugar."

After a few days at the mission station at Rotorua he headed for Lake Taupo and was very impressed by Horohoro: "It formed the boundary of the plain as perfectly as if it had been a straight wall . . . a perpendicular wall of basaltic rock, rising to about 2000 feet from the surface of the plain." Bidwill made the first ascent of Mount Ngauruhoe on his own because his Maoris were fearful of tapu. The mountain was in eruption and the scene desolate: "A circular plain of sand at the north-east base would have been a fitting scene for the wildest piece of *diablerie* that ever entered the brain of a German, or was embodied by his pencil . . . The cone is entirely composed of loose cinders, and I was heartily tired of the exertion before I reached the top. Had it not been for the idea of standing where no man ever stood before, I should certainly have given up the undertaking." He noted that it was lucky for him that another eruption did not take place when he was climbing up a watercourse, else he ". . . should have been infallibly boiled to death". He gave a graphic description of the crater: ". . . the most terrific abyss I ever looked into or imagined. The rocks overhung it on all sides, and it was not possible to see above ten

The bluffs of Horohoro were familiar to early travellers between Rotorua and Taupo. Today their approaches have been graced by fertile pasture land.

Mount Ngauruhoe in eruption. It was fortunate for the botanist J. C. Bidwill, who first climbed the mountain, that the volcano was relatively quiet on his visit.

yards into it from the quantity of steam which it was continually discharging." He did not remain on top for long because he "... heard a strange noise coming out of the crater, which I thought betokened another eruption". He descended because he "... did not wish to see an eruption near enough to be either boiled or steamed to death".

The visit by Henry Williams to Taupo coincided with a visit by the Wesleyan missionary, James Buller, who referred to "... climbing hills, threading forests, wading streamlets" and the "... wild scenery of that inland sea". He noted: "After leaving Kawhia, I did

not sleep in a bed again until my return to the north. We had skirted the plains of the Waikato; we had seen the fertile valleys lying between Pirongia and Kakepuku; and, from many an elevation, we had had command of a glorious prospect." By January 1840 Buller was down at Pipiriki on the Wanganui river. These inland Maori tracks to and from Taupo were followed by several parties whose reports aroused great interest in the thermal and lake regions. Richard Matthews's trip from the Wanganui and Ohura to the Mokau and beyond to the Waipa was another remarkable effort.

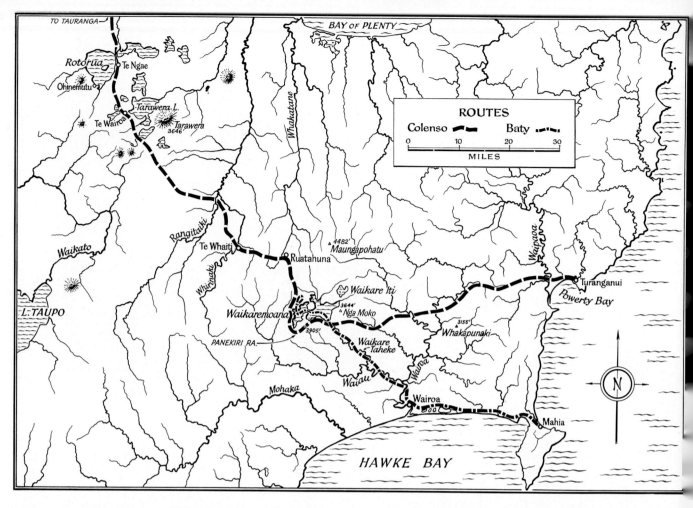

If the relations between the Anglicans and the Wesleyans were good because of their mutual tolerance, the same could not be said of the relations between Anglicans and Roman Catholics. In December 1841 there was a vigorous clash between William Colenso of the Church Missionary Society and Father J. W. Baty at Lake Waikaremoana when their trails crossed from entirely different quarters. Both men were interesting in their own right and Colenso, in particular, has a special niche in Hawke's Bay exploration that will be explained in the next section.

Colenso, a Cornishman, was a layman and printer with the Paihia mission at the Bay of Islands in 1834. He was also a fine botanist and enterprising explorer. Father Baty was also a fine botanist and enterprising explorer. Father Baty was serving a term under his Bishop Pompallier and operated from Wairoa. In this era of long walks Colenso undertook a real marathon. His journey began in Poverty Bay and took him to Lake Waikaremoana, thence to Rotorua, Auckland and the Bay of Islands. The most important part from the point of view of exploration was the area around Lake Waikaremoana. He relished his experiences and wrote: "Gaining the summit of the high hill before me, I had an extensive view of the interior. Hill rose on hill (Pelion on Ossa) in continuous succession as far as the eye could reach. To the left

was Whakapunake [Whakapunaki] (the fabled residence of the gigantic moa), an immense table-topped hill, or rather mountain; while to the right, far away in the distance Panekire, a peculiarly precipitous mountain, cast its bold outline in fine relief into the sky. This, my Maori guide informed me, was Waikare, to which place we were going."

In the meantime, and unknown to Colenso, Father Baty was approaching from the south. Weirs in the Waikare-Taheke stream had hampered canoe travel but Baty's company of thirty Maoris was experienced in such country: "The way led over the hills, and they had to scramble along steep sidelings, by the narrow track through bush and forest and fern-clad gulches, until the river was again met and they were face to face with a dangerous ford." Father Baty saw the remains of a cannibal oven. On 23 December he reached the village on the shore of Lake Waikaremoana, where boisterous weather barred progress for a few days. Baty's chronicler, the Rev. J. Hickson, recorded: "On Christmas Eve, a Protestant missionary from the Bay of Islands came on the scene, and launched a personal attack in wordy warfare on the priest and his followers, but his invectives made absolutely no impression." Colenso's account also referred to a strong wind making it impossible to cross the lake, and he described himself as a prisoner,

At Ruatahuna in the Urewera country. This view of Maungapohatu from Rua's house shows
the extent to which the Tuhoe tribe had cleared land. When Colenso visited this place in 1844,
the kainga of Toratai was significant; it is likely that it was located in the clearing
high on the left.

25

spending a most unpleasant Christmas. Colenso's journal, written in the bush, noted that when he met Father Baty "in his Black Habit" they exchanged civilities without shaking hands, and argued their theological doctrines for three hours. No doubt the Maoris were entertained, being themselves experts at disputation. There was another such debate between Colenso and Father Baty a week later, which Colenso won, according to his journal. It is a pity that these explorers were divided by their pieties, because as travellers with Maori guides they were both enduring and enterprising. Baty's account at times became lyrical: "Close at hand but two thousand feet below, were the dark blue waters of Waikare-Moana, with the gleaming white cliffs of Panekiri [Panekire] and the massive range of Nga Moko [Ngamoko] over-hanging . . . range after range of mountains merging into the Kaingaroa Plains to the west. . ." Like Colenso, Father Baty spent some time in printing religious works in Maori; unlike him he died at forty years, worn out (it was said) by his labours and his privations.

As Colenso continued his journey over ranges to the west he was constantly delighted by new botanical finds. The second to last night of 1841 was stormy: "The heavy rain and rattling hail which unceasingly poured down; the vivid lightning and hollow-sounding thunder reverberating awfully in neverending echoes among the hills; the angry winds that furiously rushed in fitful roaring blasts through the ancient forests, rocking and creaking, and, lashing the monarchs of centuries as so many saplings of a year, stripping their 'leafy honours' and cracking off their branches, hurled them to the earth; the hooting of owls and shrieking of parrots, which flew affrightedly about, seeking shelter — all united to declare, in a voice too plain to be misunderstood, the great com-motion nature was undergoing — fit knell for the departing year!"

To add to the gloom of incessant rain, the only guide deserted Colenso's party, which consisted of Maoris from distant parts. Colenso explained his dilemma to his Maoris, who agreed to trust to his compass to find a way to the next village. To their amazement they were overtaken by their deserting guide who had gone back to Waikare and returned to Colenso with a load of potatoes. So they reached the remote village of Ruatahuna. Colenso was ". . . busily engaged with the natives, many of whom were astonished at seeing a white man". Colenso's route continued, passed Te Whaiti and from a hill above the Whirinaki river he brooded on the scene: ". . . not a human being dwelt in all that immense tract of country on which my eager gaze then rested. The grass grew, the flowers blossomed, and the river rolled, but not for man. Solitude all!"

At the Rangitaiki the fording was made by holding tent poles and crossing obliquely — a method that was to become standard practice among exploring goldminers in the south twenty years later. By the time that Colenso reached his destination in the Bay of Islands he had collected nearly 1,000 specimens in natural history of which he considered that some 600 were new.

1842 saw a long walk by the scientist Dr Ernst Dieffenbach and Captain William Symonds from Kawhia to Taupo and beyond. Maori tapu prevented them from attempting Mt Ruapehu. Bishop Selwyn and Chief Justice William Martin later that year began a journey of spectacular length, from the Manawatu to Auckland via Hawke's Bay and the East Coast. For the purposes of this section, the first crossing of the Raukumara Range was truly explora-tion. Another missionary, the Rev J. W. Stack, joined Selwyn, Martin and their Maori guides, with food, hatchets and knowledge of an old Maori war-trail to the Bay of Plenty. Wading and walking up the Waiapu valley was prelude to a long bush climb

Lake Waikaremoana from Panekire. The waters of this inland mountain lake can be turbulent in storms.

North Island
NEW ZEALAND

Scale of Miles

50   0   50   100   150

Routes

Marsden: ....
Selwyn: − − − − −
Colenso: ————
Dieffenbach: ....

North Cape

Kerikeri   Bay of Islands

Whangarei

Dargaville

Kaipara Har.

Auckland

Manukau Harb.

Thames

Waikato R.

Raglan H.   Tauranga

Kawhia H.   Te Awamutu

Rotorua

Bay of Plenty

East C.

New Plymouth

Taupo

Gisborne

L. Taupo

Wairoa

Poverty B.

Ngaruahoe

Mt Egmont

Ruapehu

Hawke Bay

Mahia Pen.

Napier

C. Kidnappers

Manawatu R.

Otaki

Castlepoint

Wellington

C. Palliser

Cook Strait

South Pacific Ocean

Bishop Selwyn

Selwyn and another missionary sit on a log while George Clarke, protector of aborigines, speaks to a Maori gathering. Selwyn made this sketch in 1842.

27

The rugged barrier of the Raukumara Range crossed at some point by Selwyn and his party from the East Coast to the Bay of Plenty.

and the carrying of water to a high camp. The subsequent crossing of the range and the steep descent to the Raukokore was trying. Selwyn revived his tired porters by making them a medicine he called rongoa, composed of boiled water with chocolate, flour and sugar to nourish and warm tired men sleeping in damp surroundings.

The next day's tramp down the Raukokore, through a gorge only seven feet wide and to which the sun never penetrated, led to a climb over another saddle, beyond which improvised rope had to be used on the descent. Stack became ill and had to be carried on a stretcher. They reached Te Kaha on the coast on 10 December, and Tauranga on 17 December. Selwyn's long walk had included riding $86\frac{1}{2}$ miles, canoeing 249 miles, and walking 762 miles. The journey across the Raukumaras, which comprised some of the key parts of the whole Visitation Tour, has seldom been repeated. Geoff Wilson and Norman Elder, both renowned travellers and historians of the North Island ranges, ninety years later, also found

the route from the Raukokore to the Bay of Plenty hazardous because of the steep papa cliffs. It is likely that development for hydro-electricity will eventually open up some of this country with tracks and huts.

In fact one must not overlook the fact that when the initial reconnaissance journeys had been made, whether by missionaries, traders or scientists, the next stage was a surveyor with the responsibility of mapping the country. The surveyors were usually self-reliant to the point that they carried their loads themselves and did not need guides. While they found that the Maoris looked sideways at such peasant-like behaviour, they were all the better for their independence. In 1843 R. Harrison and one Robinson reached Taupo from the Wanganui. Colenso had liked his taste of exploring and late in 1843 he returned to the Lake Waikaremoana country for the stimulus of storms and to provide Selwyn with figures of a census of the Tuhoe and other inland tribes. But Colenso was by now looking backward to his tradesman's tasks of printing the Gospel and looking forward to

28

The Ohakune approach to Ruapehu. The Onetapu Plain lies on the far side of the mountain beyond the skyline.

his future as itinerant deacon and explorer, as related in the following section.

Another Anglican stalwart was the Rev Richard Taylor. His approaches to the central plateau and the volcanic mountains of the North Island were well described in his journal and may be compared with certain entries by Donald McLean as "Chief Protector of Aborigines". In 1844 Taylor was the first European at the head of the Wanganui. He wrote: "I felt much fatigued but as I am the first European who ever trod this road I must not repine," but another entry had the rather doleful comment: "A rainy night and morning, I awoke with a sharp attack of rheumatism." The travelling must indeed have been tough: ". . . a very wet and dirty walk we had the path being either very slippery or rough with the trees fallen across, it was either up or down and so wet. We ascended Taumatamaue which is more properly speaking a long mountain ridge very fatiguing to climb, and then about 6½ [6.30 p.m.] to our resting place at the junction of two rivers the banks

were perpendicular rocks full fifty feet high down and up which we managed to get by means of native ladders."

Taylor was quite captivated by his sight of Tongariro: "We had a lovely view of Tongariro from the summit of the mountain we were standing on whose base is washed by the Wanganui, the boundary is indeed a noble mountain and beautiful as Taranaki is, in size and elevation it will bear no comparison to this." Taylor could evoke the feeling of the country he described: "We passed over the Onetapu a sandy plain or rather one of cinders and vitrified blocks of stone intersected by deep ravines . . . This plain is most dreary, no birds, nothing but the dismal rushing sound of the blast."

Like his fellow missionary explorers Taylor found some of the Maori tracks quite hair-raising: "We descended two bad paths down a cliff full 400 feet nearly perpendicular and ascended two cliffs equally bad one I think was as bad and dangerous as any I ever ascended, it was up a slippery clay stone part of

29

DEACCESSIONED

the way so perpendicular that it was more like climbing a wall, the last part was the worst being loose gravel which gave way when trod upon." This particular March (1845) Taylor's party approached the village of Inland Patea. Taylor described Ruapehu as ". . . a gloomy looking mountain the heat of its sides not allowing the snow to rest upon it". In November he was again describing the central plain: "Nothing grew on it, it reminded me of a world blasted by sin even the thorn and the brere [briar] were wanting, and I was very thankful to get over it as the high cold wind blew the ashes into our eyes and this together with the softness of the soil rendered it very difficult to walk upon." Donald McLean's version was: "A heavy oppressive day, over volcanic remains of buried cinders and lava, which is the general character of this part of the country."

For missionary travellers not dressed for mountaineering some of the experiences must have been distressing and it is a wonder that there were no recorded deaths by exposure. The matter-of-fact way in which officials as well as missionaries could now travel in the North Island still underlined their debt to Maori trails and Maori guides. Perhaps also the thoughts about New Zealand landscape and bush were changing. Memories could remind a settler of other lands: "There was not such a thing as a tree on either side to relieve the eye, nothing but these interminable Hills covered with Fern. I could not help fancying that the scenery would bear a strong resemblance to the Highlands of Scotland." The condemnation already quoted: "It has many, many times been grief to mind to see thousands of acres of land lying waste and miles of country desolate and entirely uninhabited" had given place to a fuller and more prophetic understanding: "It will be the work of human industry, aided by a singularly fine climate, to cover with the verdure of fields and lawns many millions of acres in New Zealand, over which the fern and myrtle at present hold undisputed sway; and this task accomplished, the scenery of New Zealand will be as rich and as inviting as that of any country in the world."

Surveyors of course had the heavy end of the stick, because they had to live in the back country as well as travel in it. Yet this element of hardship in the field of pioneering gave them a ruddy health and endurance, a capacity to live off the land, a knowledge of the tricks of the swamps and the rivers, and an appreciation of bush for its own sake — a place of shelter, with good tinder for fuel, and a maze which a good compass could unravel.

It was true that essayists and some poets would continue to harp on the myth that the descendants of the pioneers were as fearful of the bush as had been their forefathers; that they would feel out of place in this alien cloak, and they would shiver on their narrow islands isolated in the far Pacific. But a robust

The Rev Richard Taylor from a crayon drawing by H. E. Hobson.

Donald McLean

Maori footwear sketched by Richard Taylor in his journal: "the pareare or sandal used as a snow shoe in the interior made of flax or the Te tree."

series of generations has in fact disproved some intellectual theories. Men have learned to hunt wild animals, to tramp valleys, cross ranges and passes, climb mountains; to laugh at the idea that forest is alien or terrifying. The Maoris themselves had respect for bush and understood the need to conserve bird life. When the Maori wars raged they were as a fire in the fern rather than as a forest holocaust. The Pakeha warriors on the other side of the hill, such as the Forest Rangers, also adapted to the needs of bush navigation and to its essential quality of protection for guerillas.

The Rev. Benjamin Y. Ashwell, quoted elsewhere, had talent for the accurate phrase. He was moved to Old Testament vigour in this passage about the country near Horahora: "The country was desolate beyond description. Thousands of Thousands of Acres of miserable land without Tree or Shrub Water also was scarce. This plain extends to Taupo, Rotorua and almost to Ahuriri. I was forcibly reminded of the great and terrible wilderness spoken of in Scripture."

Listen further to Ashwell reporting to the Church Mission Society as he was on an overland trip to Rotorua, dependent as usual on good Maori guides: ". . . began to ascend Maunga Huiarau. The Gale had now commenced and as we neared the Summit we felt the cold exceedingly. I cannot tell the height of the lofty Mountain but I was informed that the Snow continues on it from the beginning of winter till

nearly the end of spring. We ascended and descended fifteen different summits." The party reached Ruatahuna that evening.

At a stage when few summits had been reached in Switzerland, it is interesting to contemplate high government officials in New Zealand having ambitions to do some mountaineering. The most famous of these was Lieutenant-Governor E. J. Eyre, the explorer from Australia and the Protector of Aborigines there. Eyre was sworn in on 12 January 1848 by Sir George Grey as the boss of the artificial and short-lived New Zealand province of New Munster, including the whole of the South Island and the southern part of the North Island up to the mouth of the Patea river. As Governor of New Zealand, Grey lived in Auckland. There were running sores of trouble between these two men. For the purposes of this book let us consider their quarrels on the subjects of exploration and mountain climbing.

Eyre's biographer, Geoffrey Dutton of Australia[1], gives an admirable summary of Eyre's moves at the end of 1848: ". . . Eyre saddled up horses and set off with the native interpreter, McLean, for the north coast. Rumour in Wellington, where he had kept his plans secret, had it that he was going to make an attempt on one of the two mountains towards Lake Taupo, Tongariro (6,458 ft) or Ruapehu (9,175 ft). McLean found Eyre a pleasant companion, though

[1] *The Hero as Murderer* (London, 1967) pp 180-1

A surveyor's camp, from a period engraving in the *Illustrated London News* of 1850.

E. J. Eyre in his Australian days.

he admitted in his Journal to falling asleep in the canoe while Eyre was talking. Eyre must have been a comical sight, floundering with McLean through the swamps up to their knees in water: 'The Lieutenant-Governor dressed in a tartan plaid and plaid trousers, a becoming dress for such an excursion but I thought they were not so becoming for him to wear as they should be for me.' Eyre made various friendly contacts with the Maoris, over 600 being present at one meeting. . .

"At the Wanganui mission Eyre joined the Rev. Richard Taylor, with whom he was going on to Taupo. Taylor had gone on excursions with Eyre before, and of one remarked 'I was much fatigued but Lieutenant-Governor Eyre seemed quite fresh; he is certainly a great pedestrian. . .' On 4 January they left for Taupo, but almost immediately were stopped by a policeman, the last of a chain sent puffing up the coast with orders from Grey to return immediately to Wellington."

Grey's autocratic and rude behaviour was explicit in his letter to Eyre dated 2 January 1848 here quoted from the National Archives: "Sir, I have the honour to state to your Ex. that I have received a letter [word crossed out] intelligence from Wellington to the effect that immediately after my instruction you had quitted that settlement for a period of at least six weeks with an intimation to the Senior member of your Executive Council that you did not know when you should return." Grey apparently had the impression that Eyre would remain in Wellington to adjust land claims and financial affairs; Grey himself would not have left Wellington at such a critical time (or so he wrote)". . . It now only remains for me to require your Ex. not to quit under any circumstances what

ever the limits of the Province [i.e. New Munster] entrusted to your Government." He went on to suggest that Eyre had lost the confidence of the Maori and Pakeha in his administration because of his absence.

Eyre's reply to Grey on 13 January 1849 was not so much spirited as loquacious. A return rebuff of a few lines would have sufficed, but Eyre went into a wordy examination and wrote that Grey was "impressed with the belief *First*. That [i.e. Eyre] had left Wellington with the intention of quitting the Province being absent for a period of certainly six weeks but with the prospect of my Return being indefinitely delayed." Secondly Eyre realised that Grey had charged him with neglect in making certain financial arrangements and thus had delayed the adjustment of some land questions; thirdly that Grey believed that Eyre had transferred some duties of his own to the New Munster Executive Council.

Then Eyre's defence hotted up. He tackled Grey with complaining on surmises and stated that "a calumny at least has been given" on "mere conjecture". Eyre wrote: ". . . since to no single person in Wellington, save the Gentleman who accompanied me out of Town did I impart the nature of the Tour I proposed making thro' a portion of the Province or the objects I had in view in undertaking it". Eyre claimed that even he himself did not know how long he would be absent. The tour was undertaken because although he had held office for eighteen months he had not gone further north than Otaki, with the exception of a view of Wanganui from shipboard. The objects and intentions of his temporary absence from Wellington were that he wanted to get acquainted with various tribes and to make the natives friendly to the Government.

32

Sir George Grey; the engraving by W. W. Alais was made from a photograph.

PLATE 1

What did the first travellers to New Zealand see besides the coastline? Probably Maori settlements made a great impression. This tinted lithograph of Kororareka about 1827 is by de Sainson, artist with Dumont d'Urville's ship *Astrolabe*. At this stage visiting artists confined themselves to accessible settlements on the coast.

OUR ENCAMPMENT Novᵗ 29 1845

PLATE 2
"Our encampment"; this delicate pencil sketch was made on 29 November 1845
during the expedition by Richard Taylor and Donald McLean (*see page 30*).
The sketch comes from the Alexander Turnbull Library.

In fact Eyre got along with the Maoris as well as he had with the South Australian Aborigines. Dutton comments: "Eyre made an excellent impression with the natives when Major Wyatt sent a gunboat to take Eyre across to the settlement [Wanganui]; he declined the offer, and crossed with Taylor in his little canoe, 'much to the admiration of the natives that he should send back the gunboat and *prefer* being paddled over by a native. They remarked that he was indeed their governor but that the Pakehas [white men] would be offended at his constantly staying among them!'"

Eyre's letter to Grey continued that his proposed route was in the Manawatu, the Rangitikei and so to Wanganui and Taupo. And as for his absence being indefinitely prolonged, another ten days and he would have completed his tour and his primary objectives of calming the Maoris.

A gossip of the period suggested that a fortuitous object of Eyre's tour was to climb Tongariro before Grey could do so. It would be logical for Grey to react violently against Eyre and, in forbidding him again to leave the province of New Munster, deny him access to the mountain. In the event and a few years later Grey was in the Tongariro group but the Maoris themselves used the weapon of tapu to frustrate his ambitions.

In an uncritical biography *The Romance of a Pro-Consul* a writer of 1899 described how Grey had rejected the British Constitution of 1846 and had later fashioned his own. The following account of the mapping of the new constitution purports to be in Grey's own words: "The circumstances under which I drafted it, were peculiar, not to say romantic. . . In the end, when my thoughts had bent to a shape, I went up into the mountains between Auckland and Wellington, camped on Ruapehu, in a little gipsy tent, and set to the task. . . Where did I get my inspiration? Oh, by talking to the hills and trees, from long walks, and many hints from the United States constitution." His biographer commented: "There was in it the breath of the mountains, to which he had gone, as the great law-giver of the Jews went up into them to pray."

There is another reference to this in a letter that Grey wrote in his old age to the New Zealand Alpine Club claiming an ascent of Ruapehu (probably the northern peak, Te Heu Heu): "On another occasion, the date of which I cannot recollect — but it was at the time that a new constitution was about to be given to New Zealand — I remained there for some days and had only Natives with me."

Be these things as they may, there was the evidence of one of his secretaries, Lieutenant J. J. Symonds, who travelled with him overland from Auckland to Rotorua, and Taupo to Taranaki December 1849-January 1850. Symonds wrote: "The Governor fancies himself a great bushman but fails most miserably in his New Zealand bush ideas." This was not to take any credit from Grey for considering his problems in the wilderness or to deny that he reached a point high on Ruapehu.

We have seen that Grey could obstruct expeditions such as those projected by Eyre; let us examine how he pursued his own. A pamphlet published both in English and in Maori in 1851 by G. S. Cooper, tells the story of his travels with Grey: *Journal of an Expedition overland from Auckland to Taranaki by way of Rotorua, Taupo, and the West Coast. Undertaken in the Summer of 1849-50, by His Excellency the Governor-in-Chief of New Zealand.* Cooper later became the Colonial Secretary.

The party left Auckland on 5 December 1849; it included Grey, Symonds, Cooper, an interpreter and two others. They met rain in the Thames-Waikato: "Found ourselves, on awaking this morning, lying in a pool of water, having pitched our tent in a hollow place last night." They made tarpaulins serve as cover and shelter. Cooper referred to Grey thus: "The Governor bore all our mishaps very stoically, appearing to care very little what became of that which had been provided for the inner man, but amused himself all day in his tent surrounded by natives, learning their songs, proverbs, ceremonies." He described Symonds: "The most agreeable travelling companion as well as the best bushman I have ever met with, as usual, took the lead."

Two days later (13 December) wetness abounded: "The Governor and Symonds had the advantage of us here, as being experienced bushmen, they had all their clothes packed in water-proof tin cases and were well supplied with tarpaulins. The weather was so dismal that even the natives could not keep their spirits up."

At times the Maoris were disconcerted by Grey's appearance: ". . . What had become of the Governor, as they cou'd see neither cocked hat, feathers, sword, nor silver lace on any one of the party and when His Excellency was pointed out to them they seemed quite astonished and almost disappointed at beholding a man in a common shooting jacket, a Jim Crow hat, trowsers rather the 'worse for wear and a pair of moustaches'. 'Is *this* the Governor?' they all exclaimed."

Cooper noted that ". . . the ascending Tongariro had been with the whole of us, the main object of the journey" but because of Maori tapu Grey decided to take the party down the Wanganui by way of Mokau. For some comments on the remainder of the trip we have to consult the copy of a journal fragment written by Captain Symonds and rescued by Dr T. M. Hocken. This document, now in the Hocken Library, gives valuable though disconcerting sidelights on Grey, and some depth to the nature of the travel.

On 10 January 1850 Symonds noted the day was "Very fine, the Gov. makes a speech to the natives which has the effect of causing one of them to leave his pipe behind — pass through Mangakino over a very dangerous bridge, pass through some very thick fern land." The following day it was ". . . up early and start about 5 pass through a wood about 6 miles then into rough fern, then through a very romantic valley to Tapuwae where we cross a very steep chasm almost perpendicular — this was one of Te Rauparaha's strongholds on his rereat from Waikato from which he was driven by Te Whero Whero." That day they walked twenty-six miles. On 12 January Grey was determined to start for Kawhia in spite of rain in the morning: ". . . thousands of mosquitoes all night." They crossed the ridge of Mt Pirongia.

Coastal problems gave trouble on 17 January: "Sultry, pass the dreaded Wapuku [Waipuku] & Moetara over very steep cliffs of dangerous ascents & descents such as I never wish to pass again, after a forced march reach the Hu where we encamp being unable to round the point owing to the flood tide." At the Mokau they met Waitara ". . . lately christened Te Kerei after the Gov',".

Symonds had a very forthright view of Governor Grey as a bushman. This is part of a fascinating entry of 26 January: "Torrents of rain, proceed up over another rapid Mangapohue & camp. I never will again if I can help it travel in N.Z. with Governors or other great men of any description having once felt the extreme discomfort more particularly perhaps as Gov. Grey fancies himself a great bushman but fails most miserably in his N.Z. bush ideas — he used to fancy himself in Australia & spoke of not pitching his tent at times, had he not done so everything belonging to him would have been drenched. Our camp is on the banks elevated some 30 feet above the roaring flooded river, the natives though drenched are making themselves very comfortable after their fashion, putting up sheds covered with nikau, it is most amusing to watch them, these Mokau natives seem more apt to bushing than most I have seen owing to the rough country they inhabit. The coal we passed at Wangapohue seems of some extent & it is said to be good, but the natives are too lazy to work it & the river is too dangerous to bring it down."

This description of the Mokau continued with reference to ". . . some beautiful reaches with limestone cliffs above, a pretty waterfall drops noisily into the river at a rapid".

The concluding entry on 2 February took Symonds back to his wife in Auckland: "Up with the sun & after a sharp walk over the oft described track through wood & plain arrive at Waters (?) station where I get a horse & ride to Epsom arriving about 4 & find my good little wife walking in the garden little expecting to see me. Glad to find myself at home in my snug little cottage after several weeks absence."

Dr Hocken added this postscript to his copy: "Here Cap. Symonds' journal ends — the delights of a good wife & snug cottage being apparently inconsistent with the further keeping of a journal."

The Mokau River. Contrast the idealised sketch by C. C. Clarke (*above*) in 1850 with the photograph at *left*.

Taranaki, Hawke's Bay, Wairarapa and Wellington

Emerge from the interior of the North Island, head South, and you will find local history with the honoured name of William Colenso, an increasing deference to survey parties, a respect for the needs of pastoralists, and all trails leading, if not to Rome, then to Wellington in the wind funnel of Cook Strait. By now the mountains have become lower, the plains better defined, the river gorges less spectacular. The land can become tamed, and the roving explorer scarcely gets a meal ticket by comparison with his fellows in the South Island.

A Taranaki survey camp of the eighties. Mount Egmont's cone rises proudly above the bush.

A German naturalist and a seaman-whaler were the first men to climb Mt Egmont. Neither this fact nor the date of 23 December 1839 makes them explorers. In fact many mountaineers have put exploring aside in favour of first ascents, because sometimes the conditions favour one pursuit or the other, seldom both. In this case however the naturalist Dr Ernst Dieffenbach, then twenty-eight years old and the whaler James Heberley then thirty-two years old were exploring fortuitously when they climbed Egmont.

Furthermore Dieffenbach recorded his experiences in serious scientific books which seal the regard which history can give him.

Taranaki's history rightly belongs to Maori legend and Maori tribal activities. For the Pakeha, Taranaki history began when in 1770 Captain James Cook named Mt Egmont after a First Lord of the Admiralty, and when, a year later, the French navigator named it Mascarin Peak. Dieffenbach's courage lay not so much in tackling a steep mountain but in being prepared to take the consequences of outraging Maori tapu. He did not succeed at first. Bad weather, shortage of food and dense bush defeated him. His successful climb was aided by Heberley. The Maori guides packed it in when they reached the snow: one can sympathise with a combination of bare feet cold in the snow and local tapu. Heberley led to the top, up frozen snow. A fog came down but Dieffenbach dutifully boiled water for a thermometer reading. He made good observations of Taranaki from the summit and wrote: "In future time, this valley, as well as Mount Egmont, and the open rolling land at its base, will become as celebrated for their beauty as the Bay of Naples, and will attract tourists from all parts of the globe."

If you ask how the explorers cut their way up the summit snows, the reply is that Dieffenbach had a geologist's hammer and Heberley the butt end of a gun. It is interesting to reflect that the year of this ascent was 1839; the same that saw Bidwell on the top of Ngauruhoe. What was going on in Europe at that time in its mountain world? Florence Nightingale's party from Geneva was climbing a pass on donkeys and then in a sledge covered with straw and drawn by four oxen. An English traveller was more concerned with conditions of life in Switzerland — life for travellers, that is: "The quarters are of course not of the best; however we got tolerable coffee, and good bread, butter, and milk. No fleas . . . I made my tea in a shaving pot, and washed my hands in a slop basin, and, as in the days of the patriarchs, had a sheep killed for my refection." Perhaps Dieffenbach with his Maori guides and local food was not so badly off after all. And what of the summit of Mt Egmont? Dieffenbach found the skeleton of a rat there and wondered whether it had been left by a hawk.

Dieffenbach made other journeys in New Zealand, and also visited the Chatham Islands. He later returned to Germany and became a professor of geology. There is a coincidence in the careers of Bidwill and Dieffenbach: neither spent his life in the country where young ambition had been rewarded by satisfying adventures and new botanical specimens. It must have been a great disappointment to Dieffenbach that in 1841 he was denied the first ascent of Mt Ruapehu by the Maori tapu enforced by the Maori chief Te Heu Heu, who also prohibited Hochstetter, another scientist, from going high.

Journeys in the low country in Taranaki were quite feasible. Octavius Hadfield in February 1840 made a walk of 350 miles from Otaki to Cape Egmont and back, took four weeks and met Maoris who had not seen a missionary before. Neither Hadfield nor his

biographer has been generous with details. For a likely account, turn to *Adventure in New Zealand* by E. Jerningham Wakefield who, a month later, had gone from Wanganui to Patea. His object was to see ". . . some of the natives unvitiated by intercourse with savage white men, and unimproved by missionary labours". He had borrowed eight slaves as pack-horses and noted: "The 'boys' were extremely handy in making up the bundles, which they strapped on to their backs by belts resembling braces in form, neatly plaited of flax."

Frequently in this compression of explorers' accounts one is tempted to pause and reflect on the contrast between then and now. Here is such a contrast for the traveller from Wellington to Porirua who tears along the motorway at a legal 60 mph or who sits in a railcar going too fast to allow him to read his newspaper. Read then Wakefield's account of the old Porirua trail: "After a tedious march of two or three hours over very undulating ground on the top of the range [Johnsonville], along a track constantly obstructed by webs of the kareao, or supple-jack, we came to the brow of a descent, from which we had a view of a narrow wooded valley, and a peep of the sea in Cook's Strait over a low part of the further hills. On descending the hill, we found ourselves in a fine alluvial valley, through which a considerable stream brawled and cascaded. Noble forest-trees and plenteous underwood intercepted all view of anything but the beaten track along which we progressed. Just about dusk, we emerged from the forest into a jungle of flax, shrubs and long reeds, at the spot where the stream discharges itself into an arm of the sea which forms part of the harbour of Porirua or 'Dark Pit'."

There was some trouble: the slaves refused to go past Paremata.

Off the Rangitikei coast Wakefield travelled by canoe: "When I woke once or twice during the night, the canoe was lifting over the long swell, the moon and stars shining bright and clear, and a heavy dew falling on the sleepers coiled in their blankets, and the only sound to disturb the calm of the scene was the distant roar of the surf." When the party landed near the mouth of the Wangaehu Wakefield had lost his boots in the surf. North of Wanganui the going included cliff climbing by a beaten track and a subsequent walk across sand plains to Waitotara.

Wakefield's report was generally favourable to the region he had traversed. His influence as only son of Edward Gibbon Wakefield, coloniser extraordinary, was dubious, but whether one reads his book as propaganda for the New Zealand Company or as an exuberant narrative of a frisky young fellow, it is quite an experience.

A settler of the forties barters with the Maoris who carry enormous loads. J. A. Gilfillan made this sketch.

A horseman sets out on a journey from Porirua. The drawing was published as an illustration to E. J. Wakefield's *Adventure in New Zealand*.

Wellington and New Zealand Company surveyors must now take the limelight. They varied their work in laying out towns and settlements with explorations for farming country. Occasionally a chance maverick had broken away from the pattern of the herd, such as J. Duff, who went throught the Manawatu Gorge in a whaleboat in 1840. In context it is essential to consider untraversed coastlines and new plains in the interior, known of course to the Maori, but yet to be mapped in detail.

Robert Park, Charles Heaphy, and Robert Stokes were in the vanguard in August 1840 to follow up E. J. Wakefield's enthusiasm. They had the task of surveying the coastline from Porirua to Taranaki. Park thought the most difficult part of the road line was between Port Nicholson (Wellington) and Porirua itself. He recorded that the obstacles to surveying were ". . . the luxuriance of vegetation, and the hilly and broken character of the ground and the other impediments to be met with, are now more generally obvious than on our first arrival." He considered that ". . . two small iron steam boats, of very shallow draught of water, between Wellington and Petoni would convert the first 4,000 acres of the Valley of the Hutt into a series of market gardens, occupied by a numerous population and extend cultivation to a great distance up the valley." If we can

pause for an irrelevant comment, consider Charles Heaphy's dictum about a northern rival: "Of Auckland I can say but little in praise, the country around it is covered with stunted fern for many miles, and even wood is not to be procured with facility; the land is high above the sea, and of a dry barren nature."

The coastline survey proceeded well and the party reached Wanganui after twelve days. The whole trip took nearly two months. The average of twenty miles a day is a surprising one when the pack weights of thirty pounds, or double that, are taken into account. A young Scot, W. Deans, who had travelled with the Park-Stokes party, went with a local chief around the coast from Wellington to Palliser Bay and thus to the southern perimeter of the Wairarapa. He later went to the Canterbury Plains. A letter by Deans dated 30 October 1840 gave a good account about his exploit: "Last week I made a journey on foot, accompanied by a native, to Widerup [Wairarapa] to Palliser Bay, about 40 miles to the southward from the township of Britannia [Petone], to satisfy myself of the place of which I had heard great things from the natives and really I was not disappointed. It is their property never having been sold. Would you believe it, no colonist but myself has ever been there. . .

38

"If it turns out as well as I expect after having examined it more minutely than I had an opportunity of doing on my first journey, I think I will obtain a licence and squat there with a quantity of sheep and cattle. It is free from timber and covered with tolerable herbage." Deans did not persevere with his idea of squatting in the Wairarapa as he could have had great difficulty with the New Zealand Company and the Government about rights to land. Before he settled in Canterbury he occupied land in the Wellington Bay now known as Eastbourne.

The route taken by Deans was around the coastline from Wellington Heads, fording the mouths of the Wainui and Orongorongo rivers, rounding Cape Turakirae to Palliser Bay. This long walk has survived civilisation in one sense: it still has no road around it, but it is only a matter of time before screaming tyres vie with the seagulls. In another sense it has already been well despoiled, because the section known as Fitzroy Bay to the south-west of Pencarrow has become the outlet to a sewage scheme for the Hutt Valley population.

The stretch of coastline without a road and yet close to a city is quite unusual, and before the advent of the sewage outlet it was a popular tramp for young people heading for Palliser Bay. The route comes into prominence in subsequent pages because it was used by Colenso and other travellers. It includes some traces of Maori settlements of the 1840s and has been of interest to archaeologists. As is usual with some farmlands, the owners make efforts to curb access to itinerant walkers, but for the most part energetic people can still walk from Wellington to the Wairarapa if they avoid a whiff of sewage by using a bypass over gorse- and scrub-covered spurs, and don't mind boots full of shingle once in a while.

Clearly another way had to be found in 1841. It was not too difficult, though the local explorers made heavy weather of it. The Tararua Range merged into the Rimutaka Range at the head of the Hutt valley; there must surely be a pass or so over the hill.

As the New Zealand Company had no title to vast areas to which it aspired it had perforce to examine

Lake Wairarapa from the crest of the Rimutaka Range above the Orongorongo River. Bush and scrub made the going rough; travellers preferred to walk around the coast from Wellington to Palliser Bay.

38

land accessible to Wellington. About the time that Colenso was on the way to Lake Waikaremoana, Robert Stokes and assistants left Petone: "I determined to visit Wairarapa, by the valley of the Hutt or Erratounga [Heretaunga], and to return by the Coast." Some twenty-seven miles up the Hutt valley they were ". . . within three miles of the Tararua, after having waded through it about twenty-six times, and crossing the hills slept at night on the banks of the Pakuratahi. . . The next day leaving the stream, we ascended the Remutaka, the ridge of the hills that bound the valley of Wairarapa."

The well-graded winding road of today, with the warning notices about the danger from high winds or frost surfaces, is familiar to many motorists. The Rimutaka Hill has its occasional toll of heavy snow or gales, but for the most part now few travellers would deign to look over the side of the safety fences and glance at the conglomeration of scrub and second-growth below. Yet this same place, where today there is a tea-shop, was in November 1841 a spot of adventure and excitement for Robert Stokes: "In the

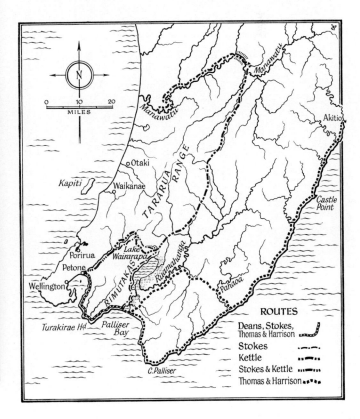

A gorge in the bush of the Tararua Ranges.

evening, while the men were engaged in preparing the tent, Mr Child and myself ascended a hill on the north-west side of the valley, and were exceedingly gratified with the prospect which presented itself. An immense plain lay at our feet, stretching to a distance of between thirty and forty miles from the head of the Lake."

Down in the Wairarapa, Stokes learnt from local Maoris that floods caused Lake Wairarapa to break its bar to the sea at comparatively regular intervals and that the Wairarapa plains gave access both to Hawke's Bay and to the Manawatu.

The journey back to Wellington was straightforward: "On our return we walked sometimes by the side of the Lake, sometimes through the bush or swamp between the Lake and the hills." When the party reached Palliser Bay and its coastline they met a storm at the mouth of the Mukamukanui — a place well-known to trampers and goat-hunters of today who call it the "Big Muks". Strata of stones loosened by rain threatened the explorers. There were dead whales near the entrance to the harbour. On 6 December the men returned to Wellington; the round-trip had taken some twelve days.

The next important venture came in August 1842 when Charles Kettle and Alfred Wills with a party of twelve men, Pakehas as well as Maoris, headed for the Manawatu and followed Jock Duff's trail through the gorge.

Kettle wrote a good description of the gorge which

The Manawatu Gorge, as painted by C. D. Barraud in 1872.

has a particular interest for the 1970s when so much effort is going into widening the goat-track that has passed as a main highway from the Manawatu to the Wairarapa and Hawke's Bay. Note that Kettle calls the gorge the pass: "The breadth of the river at the pass is reduced to 20 yards and in its bed are large masses of stone over which the water pours with great force. . . on either side the lofty rocks sometimes projected so as nearly to meet; sometimes perpendicular. . . After proceeding about half a mile through the pass, we came to a fall of fourteen feet, caused by masses of embedded rock, over which the water falls with tremendous violence." The Maoris had to haul the canoe up the river using ropes.

From the area we now call the Woodville County the exploring party headed south along the flanks of the Tararua Range. The weather was bad and the conditions cold and wet. They made abortive attempts to find the pass over the Rimutakas that Stokes had crossed, but the combination of scrubby topography and bad visibility must have beaten them. However

after a trip of thirty-two days they finally made it over the Rimutaka Hill (by a pass that was eventually used as a railway route) and to a settler in the Upper Hutt valley. Their diet of cabbage and wild pork may have been irksome but they were better found than many of their contemporaries. Their Maori leader Eahu had done excellent work. When later Kettle went on to the Otago settlement as surveyor he did good mapping work but never had hardships as he had spelt that relative word in the Wairarapa.

Selwyn and Martin would have been the next party through the Manawatu Gorge. Like Kettle, they relied on Maori canoes, and Maori porters to carry the contents above the rapids. On 12 November they headed north and thus to Hawke's Bay and the East Coast where they began their first crossing of the Raukumara Range as already noted (page 28).

There was another route from the Wairarapa to the Wellington hills apart from the coastline and the Rimutaka passes already crossed by Stokes and by

Bush on the Maori route over the Wairongomai Saddle between the Wairarapa and Wellington.

Kettle. This was the Wairongomai Saddle, an old-time Maori route. It leads from the shores of Lake Wairarapa on its western bank, up the Wairongomai stream ornamented by nikau palms and fine bush, over a low pass of some 1,200 feet and down the head of the Orongorongo river, now a source of water for Wellington City and thus barred to all travellers because of fear of contamination. The first European to cross this saddle was H. S. Tiffen, another New Zealand Company surveyor, who found his way from the Orongorongos to the valley of the Wainui-o-mata and over a ridge to Lowry Bay on Wellington Harbour.

Another event in 1843 was the forced landing at Castlepoint by the missionaries William Williams and Colenso. This mini-harbour was the point at which Colenso began his first coastal walk from the Wairarapa and along Hawke's Bay. His biographers A. G. Bagnall and G. C. Petersen give a detailed account of the vicissitudes of struggling along a coast that was interrupted by bluffs, cliffs, tidal lagoons, and rivers subject to flooding.

In April of the following year R. Harrison went from the Manawatu to the east coast of the Wairarapa but his most interesting trip was with J. Thomas in October 1844. The account was headed "Journal of a Walk Along the East Coast from Wellington to Table Cape". They left on 9 October and followed the coastal route till they reached the west bank of Lake Wairarapa, crossed the lake, and stayed at a cattle station. From one vantage point they "saw the gorge in the hills through which the road from Wairarapa to the valley of the Hutt will pass; when this is completed it will open not only Wairarapa, but all the upper country by a connected series of valleys, with the Manawatu, and on to Houriri [Ahuriri] in Hawk's Bay."

As Harrison and Thomas made their way up the coast they met small Maori settlements, streams, firewood, pastures; there were no hazards except perhaps the odd place where high tides beat against cliffs. "The walking was heavy, through high fern

41

The flat coastal shelf north of Cape Palliser gave good walking to Colenso and other travellers from Hawke's Bay.

and grass; at noon we reached Castle Point. . . there is a small harbour, which would afford shelter to two or three coasters. . . We came to a point forming a fine bay and anchorage, with a settlement and river, called Akiti [Akitio]; there is a pretty valley here which may communicate with the Manawatu."

It must be noted how essential it was for surveyors as well as for explorers to have a good eye for country. Every feature must lead to somewhere, and the approximate location of each somewhere is highly relevant to the use of a route being investigated. Some rivers on the coastal trip had to be crossed in a frail canoe. The men saw "the Rua Wahina [Ruahine] range covered with snow" from Cape Turnagain. After noting Porangahau and access to the Manawatu there was a wry note about the Maoris planting kumaras: "They are missionaries and the most notorious thieves on the coast." For "missionaries" it would be kinder to read "converts". On 30 October the final description of the interior was compelling: "Our path lay across a rugged, broken and barren country, from hence to Poverty Bay, and inland to Taupo, there is nothing but hills and mountains piled one on the other in all sorts of forms."

This theme of the complexity of ranges and ridges in the interior is a recurrent one: "The view towards the Interior was most desolate — hundreds, I may almost say 1000's of little hills, of all shapes and sizes and running to all points of compass were beneath our feet — truly the picture of 'a desart land and uninhabited.' "

It is now time to focus on the career of Colenso. At the opening of this section is the phrase: "Local history with the honoured name of William Colenso"; this links him not merely as pioneer printer, evangelistic layman, and keen botanist, but as pioneer explorer of great persistence in the Ruahine Range. This stretch of mountain country is as though it was a cross between a Canterbury shingle range and a Tararua bush complex, with gorges, mist, winter snows and misleading spurs thrown in for good measure. It is a familiar skyline boundary to motorists driving from the Manawatu Gorge to Napier. On the other side, that is the Rangitikei, it is less defined as the eye is rather bewildered by the complexity of spurs. Today it has the Napier-Taihape road to cross it.

In 1845 Colenso took up his parish as deacon of

the Ahuriri mission near Napier. The term parish is ironic, because it was bounded to the north-west by Lake Taupo, to the north by Lake Waikaremoana, to the east by the sea, to the south by Wellington. The Ruahines lay plumb in the way of travel to the west. And the area of this parish was near a quarter of the North Island.

Colenso had a human as well as a topographical interest in the Ruahines. He knew that at Inland Patea there were primitive Maori bushmen. He might not know enough Greek, Latin, or Hebrew to be able to qualify as a priest under Bishop Selwyn, but his knowledge of Maori made him far more practical as an evangelist; his energy and fortitude would carry him over and beyond rough country. He scorned a roundabout route to Inland Patea when he could make a frontal attack over the Ruahine Range. Local chiefs tried to dissuade him by tales of deaths from exposure in the snow. His guide was a former prisoner of tribal war with a memory as misty as the ranges themselves. The journey began on 4 February 1845.

Illness and rain, swamps and scrub delayed Colenso, his guide and porters. Constant fording of the rivers was cold and depressing for Pakeha and Maori alike, but Colenso was occasionally rewarded by finding new botanical specimens. Maori tracks in the scrub were narrow because the Maori walked with feet turned in. Colenso was not the first missionary to stumble awkwardly. Some days later a choice had to be made: which river gave the best route? Both were full of dead wood, stones and debris. Colenso took a narrow spur and made his height and camped on the ridge by a spring whose Maori name meant water of weariness. The guide and another Maori made an advance party to try to locate a pa and food.

So Colenso's first Sunday on the Ruahine Range was observed with a service in his open-air church, resting sore feet, combating a plague of blowflies, and waiting for the return of the scouts. He and his porters left their equipment at the spring and set out after the scouts. Sometimes they saw their traces. Other times they messed about scrub-bashing; there were no deer tracks in those days. After more climbing and a traverse of some razorbacks they arrived on the summit of the mountain known as Te Atua-o-mahuru. Colenso's biographers give an account of the panorama he would have seen: ". . . from Table Cape and Cape Kidnappers on the east coast to the central mountain mass of Tongariro and Ruapehu on the north, and beyond. To the east the whole of Hawke's Bay lay spread before them, the great forest that was later to be known as "The Forty Mile Bush" flowing down the wide valley like a green river . . . To the west was a great undulating, gorge-riven jumble of forest-covered country, the home of the isolated Patea tribe." Colenso was ecstatic, not so much because of the view but because of the profusion of new flora, ". . . all in sight at a single glance". He made his shirt a collecting bag and even the crown of his hat was pressed into service. They returned to the spring camp, where they were rejoined by the scouts who had returned with the dismal news that they were hungry, and that although they had reached a village near Patea it had neither man nor food. Loyally, they had returned to their Pakeha leader and friends.

Colenso fondled his botanical speciments that night as he folded them into protective cloths and books. Breakfast was a scatter of rice.

Without enough food to complete the crossing of the Ruahines Colenso had to pack it in. His Maoris' bare feet found the native Spaniard, speargrass, a cruel obstacle. Colenso himself had the pains of sciatica and rheumatism to discourage him. It must have been a sad party that descended by the way they had come. Mountaineers know the feeling of frustration when circumstances are against them and they have to admit defeat. Still, Colenso was gaining in experience. He would try again. But first he had to get back to his mission station on the plains. One hundred and eight fords of deep cold water and a lot of boulder-hopping were hard work. When he reached a home pa with his Maoris they were all hungry and weary.

Colenso was now thirty-four, married and with one child. He must have been very fit, because twice a year he took off for Wellington. He varied these pedestrian marathons by going inland through Hawke's Bay and the Wairarapa or around the coastline. Admittedly he had Maori porters to carry his food and gear, but whether he was following Maori trails in heavy bush or dodging tides on exposed coastal rocks or sinking into mud or sand, it was a long plod. The subsistence farming of isolated Maori pas had not yet given way to the spread of squatterdom and the ubiquity of sheep and cattle. Sometimes Colenso met with disputation, even danger, with Maori chiefs. The walk from the mission station to Wellington would take some thirty days. Part of this time would of course be spent in preaching, exhorting, instructing.

One barrier, the rocks of the Mukamuka near Cape Turakirae, was dangerous at high tides.[1] On the return trip Colenso had to swim a few feet when he was washed from the rocks.

[1] In 1855 an earthquake raised the beach level and made this passage safe.

An undated pencil sketch by Colenso. This sketch may show East Coast ranges from the mouth of the Uawa River in Tolaga Bay and could have been drawn in 1838.

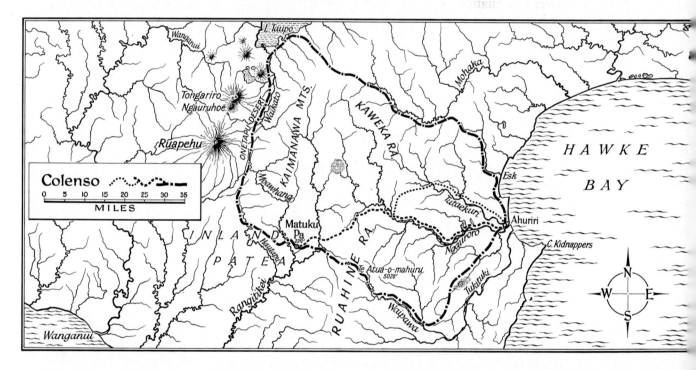

Colenso was still eager to visit Inland Patea, the elusive village beyond the Ruahines, but he had other fish to fry, his wife produced another child; his station at the Ahuriri was often beset by quarrels and uproars with Maoris; illness sometimes visited as though to stay for a long time. In February 1847 he left the mission station once again, this time for the head of the Mohaka river system. In fact he took a Maori trail that was the basis of the future Napier-Taupo road of the Pakeha. River fords in the Mohaka were swift. The missionary and his guides used the pole crossing method, on a diagonal line, which was well favoured by later explorers in the more difficult rivers of the South Island. They reached Taupo without undue troubles.

From Taupo the way lay across the desert east of Ruapehu with its exposed sands subject to rain and snowstorms. The Maoris would not retreat to Taupo; Colenso was worried about some of his plant specimens; food was short; the weather worsened. Colenso thought of the words of Ossian: "It is night. I am alone, forlorn on the hill of storms. The wind is heard on the mountain. The torrent pours down the rock. No hut receives me from the rain; forlorn on the hill of winds!." Today the traveller would make speed and his way to Waiouru for comfort and refreshments.

During a Sabbath day of rest Colenso coaxed a fire to burn and eked out the rations as best he could. He was afraid that his guide would defect.

The following day the party reached the Moawhango river, not so far from the present-day town of Taihape in the Rangitikei watershed. The going was rough and ravine-ridden. As emergency fodder they ate the tops of branches of cabbage-trees roasted over a fire and leaving a bitter flavour. Then the next day they were welcomed at an outlying village with baskets of hot potatoes. And so to the main village of Matuku, Inland Patea. Colenso described the location of this as: ". . . picturesquely situated on the ridge and summit of a very high hill, rising abruptly in the midst of these immense primeval forests which surround it for miles on every side". The panorama showed the Ruahines, Egmont, Ruapehu and Tongariro.

The inhabitants of Inland Patea were ". . . very ignorant of everything foreign (as was to be expected), but most pleasantly simple and willing to be taught". They all wore Maori mats; there was no European clothing.

Colenso was anxious to return to his station to keep a date to marry nine couples. Against the wishes of the Inland Patea inhabitants he headed for another outlying village. The beaten track led to a fearsome descent to a gorge of the upper Rangitikei river. From the village the route led through forest,

fern and scrub, and then up a riverbed filled with flood debris. The following day they met with thick fog on the tops, struggled through bad scrub and stunted beech forest, and lay down to sleep, too tired even to make camp. They had seen the skeleton of a Maori gripped in scrub who had died in a snow-storm. Four hours climb another day took them through mist to the same summit, Te Atua-o-mahuru, that Colenso had reached in 1845. They left this top of 5,000 feet and found the track to the east and to the spring in the bush. Alas this was dry, but they found water further down the ridge. Late in the evening they descended to the riverbed and Colenso knew he had at last crossed the Ruahine Range. As usual he had found some superb botanical speci-mens, including the mountain buttercup of those parts.

On the familiar trek down river Colenso and his party made good time, and was able to keep his appointment to marry the nine couples.

He made other crossings of the Ruahine Range between 1847 and 1852, survived rheumatism, and led a long and useful life on Maori linguistic and botanical research, with incursions into politics. Young men of other generations followed the Colenso footsteps over the Ruahines: among them George

William Colenso, c. 1860

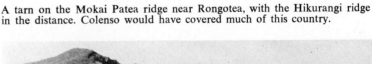

A tarn on the Mokai Patea ridge near Rongotea, with the Hikurangi ridge in the distance. Colenso would have covered much of this country.

Lowe, who later earned fame for his support to Ed Hillary on Mount Everest.

Thirteen years after he had made his long walk from the Manawatu to the East Coast and across the hills to the Bay of Plenty, Bishop Selwyn made another journey, this time south from the mouth of the Waikato river to Taranaki. His companion, Charles Abraham, teacher and church dignitary, was a good diarist as well as a close friend of Selwyn. Details of this journey were published as *Journal of a Walk with the Bishop of New Zealand from Auckland to Taranaki in August 1855.*

When they left Auckland Abraham found his pack too heavy for him at 30 lbs. This burden was called pikau in Maori. For most of the subsequent journey one of the Maoris carried it for him. There were plenty of amusing incidents in those pre-motorway days: a high tide flowing up a creek by a survey line at Onehunga and the Bishop falling into it; crossing a swamp on fallen trees under water. Sand-walking gave the Bishop raw heels. When Abraham first saw Egmont ". . . overhanging Taranaki. . . sparkling in the sun" he compared it with Mont Blanc which he had seen twenty years before from Geneva. He compared the going variously with the coast of Devon and the Isle of Wight, and described the continual changes as those ". . . from ridge-paths and table-land to woods; up and down, high and low, sandy beach, cliffs and rivers". They were never more than a couple of miles from the coast.

Sometimes the route lay ". . . up the side of a high hill, covered with forest trees of every variety of colour and shape, started with luxuriant fern trees on the slopes. Of course, the ascent involved a descent through the forest on the other side; and though this is difficult walking, from the slippery paths and the tanglement of the roots and supplejack, yet it changes the muscles." It this is not so much as exploration, the account should be studied for the excellent description of the former explorer Selwyn: "The Bishop was in his element; springing from one [rock] to another like a schoolboy; laughing and joking, scrambling and clinging on, like a sailor to a mast." The two men joked in German, quoted Latin tags at each other, and had the good sense to turn back to safe ground when the Maori guide led them ". . . up a winding precipice, where no path was visible, and the landslips had made all uncertain" an hour before sunset.

At another place, Abraham noted: "We had to dig our way with our hands, and feet, and sticks, along a crumbling slippery goat's path. The Bishop was pioneer, and did the hard work, as usual; and I certainly could not help amusing myself with the thought of some of the good people in England, who complained of the Bishop not visiting the West Coast oftener, trying the experiment of a Visitation this way. I pictured to myself the complainants holding on by their hands and nails to this crumbling crag, 500 feet overhanging the sea; and when they slipped, catching hold of the grass which cuts your hand like a knife."

Abrahams made some pertinent comments on nights in camp: "The Bishop assured me that nothing gave you a better night's rest than having been waked up in the middle. . . The great treat was, when you could pitch a tent on the sand, and could dig out a little hole for your hip to lie in." On one cliff trail the party had to use ". . . the rope-ladder, which is

Cliffs obstructed travelling on the Taranaki coast between the Mokau and Waitara.

rather a formidable affair, as it consists merely of flax leaves tied together; and you have to pull yourself up a sheer precipice of rock by it".

The bugbear of the march, the "Pari-ninihi (Slanting Cliffs), of which chalk-looking clay" proved to be better than had been expected. This was below Mokau. "We heard continually of the rope descent, 150 feet perpendicular, and I was prepared for my hands being sacrificed, in going down the rope like a sailor, of which the Bishop, being a skipper, thought little. Like most other apprehended dangers, it turned out a molehill instead of a mountain. A landslip had occurred, and the descent by rope was only twenty feet, and not more difficult than going down the side of a man-of-war into a boat."

At Waitara the party slept in a pa: "I had never been inside a regular pa before, and next morning was struck with its character. Having a high stockade of forest timbers all round, and standing on two or three acres of ground, it is all broken up within into small squares, where separate families reside; all strongly fenced and connected by narrow passages, well adapted for defence. Once in the middle, it is like a labyrinth to find the way out, or from one house to another."

Abraham's final journal entry, after the walk of 245 miles, was in a reflective vein: "We rested quietly, and gave our sore feet time to recover, while we thoroughly enjoyed looking over the beautiful scenery of this country. The mountain, in all its glorious diadem of snow, sending down such healthy bracing breezes day and night as speedily restored our strength, and added to the *bush* appetite that we had brought with us. Instead of the old proverb, 'Good wine needs no *bush*', the Bishop always reads it, 'Good bush needs no wine'; and certainly its effects are lasting and most exhilarating — I have been quite ashamed of my appetite. I feel as if I have a lee-way of a fortnight's bush-fare to make up, over and above the stimulating effects of this delicious climate."[1]

This account shows that Englishmen were acclimatising to bush travel and that in getting their second-wind, as it were, they could appreciate the benefits of tramping as well as recognise the hardships.

Before taking leave of the North Island for the unexplored regions of the South Island it is well to consider a long journey made by the surveyor and Maori scholar Percy Smith. In 1858 he had just been promoted from cadet to assistant surveyor. Survey work in the North Island was subject to constant danger, and Percy Smith got into the habit of ". . . carefully scanning every flax bush or other vantage point before passing it for fear an enemy might be in hiding with gun ready to pot me". His account is titled *Notes of a Journey from Taranaki to Mokau, Taupo, Rotomahana, Tarawera, and Rangitikei, 1858.*

This journey had first been discussed on the top of Mount Egmont. The party of five men left New Plymouth on 4 January.

Most of the pack weights were over 40 lbs a man: the contents were ". . . biscuits, bacon, sugar, choclate [*sic*], salt, spare clothes, a blanket, and a book or two". Early in the trip the problem of river fording

[1] For this and the subsequent account I am indebted to Nancy Taylor's fine editing of *Early Travellers in New Zealand* (Oxford, 1959).

A bush interior in the North Island. This sketch was made in 1919 but its timeless message carries a profusion of species that should be protected from the ravages of fire and milling.

arose. At one place Percy Smith wrote of a discussion about the best way of fording: "One proposed to make a raft; another, to swim, and float our packs on logs." As it turned out they paid three Maoris to ferry them in a canoe for three shillings. North of Urenui they had to cover four miles in less than an hour because the tide was coming in, ". . . no joke with 40 lbs. at one's back". The Parininihi cliffs were an obstacle to them, as they were to Selwyn and Abraham: "We were now under the white cliffs (Parinini), which towered above to the height of 900 feet, nearly perpendicular. Near the end of them, we had to haul ourselves up about 20 feet by a rope, and then climb the cliff for about 200 feet, which we found very hard work."

At the Mokau they hired two Maori guides to take them to Taupo and back for £10: "It was too much but rather than not go, we agreed to give it." Percy Smith noted that "The scenery of the Mokau is certainly very picturesque; but one soon gets tired of it. It sadly wants a few rocks to add boldness to it. . . The Mokau makes the most extraordinary turns, which may be accounted for by the broken country through which it runs." Thirteen miles from the mouth of the river the high tide point was reached. Smith thought that a light steamer could get up the river as far as this.

For a time the river journey was uneventful, broken only by visiting old Maori settlements, shooting wild birds, and the occasional climb. From one high hill, marked by a Pakeha's grave on top, the party took bearings to Mts Egmont, Tongariro and Ruapehu.

Percy Smith, like the missionaries of an earlier generation, found that the combination of swamps and rain was worse than wet fern: "However, there was no use in grumbling, so we pushed on, having first taken in a reinforcement of biscuit, through some most dreadful swamps, in which some of our party were near bringing their travels to a premature end. I, for my part, had the greatest difficulty in getting one of my legs out, which had gone down an immense depth, and it was not till after repeated tugs that I at last succeeded." He wrote with keen observations about the isolated Maori people met, such as the widows of two men who had taken to the bush "probably tired of the conventionalities of Maori life". He was sometimes impatient; as a young man of eighteen he found customs of tapu irritating: "Sometimes we might cook our meat inside the house, but not our choclate, and visa versa [sic]; we must not stick our knives in the wall, nor hang up our pannikins, for fear of some harm coming to the owner of the place, &c."

On 16 January they climbed "the Puketapu mountain", cleared of scrub on the top, and descended into rain. All the time Smith was taking topographical notes and bearings as befits a young surveyor. Some entries are reminiscent of the wry humour of Thomas Brunner in the Buller. Percy Smith wrote: "Passed a most dreadful night, all of us cramped and doubled up like fowls about to be roasted. The rain continued pouring down in torrents all night long, with terrific thunder and lightning. Our blankets this morning weighed about 5 times as much as they did the day before, and most of our things were wet."

Remember that in those days travellers had no waterproof sleeping-bags, nylon tents, good parkas or oilskins. When you got wet you remained wet until you had steamed yourself dry in the sun or in front of a fire. Small wonder that rheumatism afflicted many pioneers in their old age.

The first view of the inland sea, the "great Lake Taupo" gave them reason for a hearty cheer, and a run towards the lake that sobered to a walk, because it was still five miles distant. Percy Smith fainted from "fatigue, want of sleep, and hunger" when he reached Pukawa pa. T. S. Grace, the missionary and Te Heuheu, paramount chief of Ngati Tuwharetoa, gave hospitality to the party. There were diversions, as on 19 January, when they heard "a great row outside" and learned ". . . it was old Te Heuheu administering a little 'supplejack sauce' [a thrashing] to his women, who had not got up so early as usual".

There is an interesting comment about the grave of the former Te Heuheu (brother of their host) who had died in 1846 when thermal activity had buried a pa at Te Rapa. Smith wrote that the body of Te Heuheu had lain in state at Pukawa for three or four years, and then "was eventually carried half way up Tongariro, and there buried. It was to have been deposited on the top, but, owing to the inclemency of the weather and the strong winds, they had to leave him half way up." We must realise how strongly this happening would have influenced the Taupo Maoris to impose a tapu on Tongariro mountain.

A long journey around the shores and above the headlands of Lake Taupo led Percy Smith to the observation that "One of the great evils of New Zealand travelling is the scarcity of portable food." He advised future travellers to start a month or so later because the new potatoes, the principal food of the interior, were far from ripe inland in January. One day the party travelled twenty-two miles, ". . . the most we had as yet accomplished in a day. Owing to the laziness of our guides, we had never travelled so much in a day as we expected on starting."

PLATE 3
John Gully made this painting of Mt Egmont and New Plymouth sometime between 1852 and 1863. It shows the settlement and the Taranaki country clearly and comes from the album of Lady Gore Browne. (*National Archives.*)

PLATE 4

Captain William Mein Smith, surveyor-general to the New Zealand Company, made this painting of the cliffs between Te Kopi and Watarangi in Palliser Bay. The foreshore under the cliffs was the route for explorers such as William Colenso walking between the Wairarapa and Hawke's Bay. (*Alexander Turnbull Library.*)

Still on the subject of food, Smith gave his method of making damper, a kind of flapjack, from flour: "Over a hole, about two feet long, one deep, and one broad, were placed six sticks, upon which were put the dampers, and under them were hot coals from a fire alongside. In about an hour we had plenty of good damper — quite as good as if it had been cooked in the best oven in the country . . . We walked 27 miles today — no joke with sore feet and a hot sun."

For some days the party visited various lakes, pas and thermal areas, and friendly mission stations between Taupo and Rotorua. On 1 February Smith noted: "We had now been a month away from home, and our friends must have expected us, as we were to have been back by this time ["my leave of absence has expired"][1]; but there is no use depending on New Zealand travelling, for you never arrive at your destination at the time you expect." Another entry noted: "Tongariro looks beautiful from here it is really a very fine mountain but most of us did not think it so fine as Mt. Egmont"[2] In fact Tongariro, in this context, would have been Ngauruhoe.

The party made the return trip to Taranaki via the Rangitikei country. This took them past places known to today's motorists as Waiouru, Makohine, Ohingaiti. They reached their homes on 3 March "having walked 500 miles, canoed 46, and ridden on horseback 60".

This experience was very valuable to Percy Smith. His subsequent career took him to the top of his profession, as surveyor-general of the Department of Lands and Survey thirty-one years later. Even more significantly, his retirement saw him embark on a series of publications based on his knowledge of the Maori language and the history of the Maori people. His direct contact with Maori elders gave him at first hand the raw material for his scholarly studies. Although some modern archaeologists disagree with Percy Smith's conclusions they cannot ignore his findings.

We can say that by the 1860s the only pieces of minor exploration left for future generations were some tributary rivers and scrubby ridges in ranges such as the Tararuas, the Ruahines and the Kaimanawaws. The growth of good tramping clubs; the increasing activity of hunters of goats, pigs and deer; the prospecting for mineral resources; the need for good

maps for land use: all these things have encouraged the Department of Lands and Survey to push on with detailed contour maps prepared from aerial photographs and photogrammetric work. Men such as Piet van Asch of Hastings have pioneered with aerial mapping techniques and have played an important role in taking the frontiers of knowledge beyond the necessarily limited horizons of the explorers. Nor must we forget the continuing debt to the resourceful Maori explorers who were so adept at bush travel, so sensible in their ideas about conservation of both forest and bird life, and so generous to the stray Pakehas who would reap the credit and the glory as explorers in local and regional histories.

The changing attitude too must be born in mind. An observer in 1840 could write sadly of the Bay of Islands about the absence of trees. These early travellers demanded the comfort of country recognisable as Home, or, if not Home, then with some characteristic of home: "We rested at Arititaha [Aratiatia] 30 miles from Otawhao. The Scenery, here picturesque, the high ridges of Maungatautari, a lofty Mount which are densely wooded appeared close to us and the country also being studded with woods gave it the appearance of a beautiful Park, the Hills of Rangitoto and Arowena bounded our view." This missionary journal extract, also of 1840, shows a sense of order: the concept of a park is ornamented fortuitously with good-sounding Maori place-names. For future generations such names would have the same nostalgia for the New Zealand expatriate as the names Windsor Park or Windermere would have had for the colonist a hundred years before.

What was barren, bleak, and unrewarding to an early generation became the familiar contours of the backdrop to the home paddocks of succeeding ones. These familiar contours in turn built up emotive attachment. Bush to one man may seem an uncouth obstacle; to another it may be the source of inspiration and of serenity.

Another way of stating this is that some of the Maori respect and affection for the land as a place of spiritual refuge had rubbed off on to the Pakeha who had come to terms with the endurance and resource demanded by the bush. The Maori had been a guide in a spiritual sense as well as a topographical one. If exploration means learning to understand, the exploration of New Zealand's North Island was indeed an accomplished fact within fifty years of settlement.

[1] and [2]: Manuscript diary entries not in published journal.

Cook Strait at sunrise from the summit of Mount Stokes in the Marlborough Sounds. The outline of the North Island is clear and shows the Capes Terawhiti and distant Turakirae.

The Top of the South Island

Draw a line across the South Island from Kaikoura to near Greymouth; make squiggles in that line, and you have above it the three contrasting areas now to be explored. Nelson is another name for coastal and inland fertility; rich land in a superb climate. The top end of the West Coast is covered with beech forest, rent by river gorges and bounded by cliffs and a coast with but one harbour. Marlborough has wide, long expanses of native tussock, rocky mountains and some bush. There are good names among the explorers of this region, but none better than Thomas Brunner, for one of his journeys was the great journey; his equal was Kehu, his Maori guide.

Let this journey fall into context. First pause to consider why men risked death by drowning or starvation. Early settlers with their grip on the coastline had land for cultivation and pasture, but as their numbers grew the demand for land increased and spurred men on to seek more. The ranges were always barriers, but they could be crossed. It is no coincidence that in the top of the South Island the explorers were surveyors or farmers. Beyond the ranges lay more ranges, linked by ridges of rock or bush or both; below them valleys with swift rivers. To penetrate this country man needed a greater stimulus than monetary reward, a courage greater than the ordinary. Their innate qualities had to include the patience to endure the routine disciplines of swagging and camping without good shelter, and the ingenuity to stay alive when food was short, rivers flooded and exhaustion close. Time and schedules of transport did not exist; railcar whistles and lorry tyre scrunches did not exist; sometimes the future did not seem to exist for men living for each hour of the day.

The settlement of Nelson by the New Zealand Company in 1841 was a hit-or-miss affair so far as the amount of land available was concerned. Three ships with settlers anchored to the west of Tasman Bay, rather like scientists with theories but no hypotheses. This was all very well for Captain Arthur Wakefield, agent for the Company, but Frederick Tuckett, chief surveyor, had the urge as well as the professional obligation to explore.

The discovery of Nelson Harbour cleared up any doubts about the best location for the centre of settlement. Tuckett and another found the Waimea plain but did not think its area was large. Charles Heaphy entered exploration history modestly by heading for Riwaka. There will be more of Tuckett in Otago history, while Heaphy will shortly be linked with Thomas Brunner and others.

In March 1842 Tuckett probed across Golden Bay to West Wanganui and although he was unenthusiastic about the possibilities for farming he rejoiced at the "grand elements of prosperity": coal, lime, iron and timber. By November that year the assistant surveyor J. S. Cotterell made the first decisive journey with three companions amid great public interest. They sought land beyond the skyline of the hills that encompassed the Waimea plain. The party found a good pass to the Wairau: Tophouse. The Wairau valley was clearly good pasture land. On reaching the coast the men followed it south-west to the Awatere and the undulating country to the west of Cape Campbell. They reached the Clarence river but found it unfordable. The return journey was made in a whaleboat from the Wairau mouth. The Nelson settlers rejoiced.

Nobody seemed to be worried that the pass to the Wairau was 1,852 feet high or that the distance to the new land was considerable. The local newspaper reported: "Independently of the valley of the Wairoo [Wairau], there is, we believe, another and much larger one extending a considerable distance into the interior, if not throughout the length of the island, of which there are vague reports."

This was a bit of wishful thinking fostered by vague Maori reports of a large grassy plain in the interior. In January the following year Cotterell, two men and a Maori took three weeks' provisions and swagged to Tophouse, where the configuration to the south-west led them over "horrible swamps, rushes, prickles and briers" to a lake (Rotoiti) filling a valley with an outlet as a source of a river (the Buller) that proved later to flow to the Tasman Sea. They travelled to the east of the lake, but instead of finding a grassy trail they had to endure "all the warring elements — wind, rain, hail, snow, fire and smoke driving through the tent" and later pushed up the Travers river with its scrub and bush. Cotterell and a companion, appropriately Dick Panter, climbed through beech forest and over steep shingle to the crest of the St Arnaud Range with its snow beds and rocky crags. They saw a great expanse of snowy and rocky mountains in their panorama from the top, plenty of rivers and valleys, even gorges. As for great grassy plains: where where they? Would further exploration of the Buller provide any answer?

The Wairau valley proved to be a bitter consolation prize. In the course of survey work the New Zealand Company men had somewhat alarmed the Maori landowners. Nelson magistrates sent a party to arrest the obstructionists and the affray between the settlers and the Maoris that shed unnecessary blood on both sides became known as the Wairau massacre. Nelson

The St Arnaud Range from Mount Robert above Lake Rotoiti. Such ranges were barriers to explorers from Nelson.

people were angry with the survivors of the affray who had not stayed to fight it out at their leader's side, and it was natural for them to be as angry with the Maoris because at that time few Pakehas realised the reverence that Maoris had for land. They were indignant that Government action and reprisals were harmless to the rebels, if that was what they were. The setback to Nelson and its settlers was very evident. Yet so far as exploration was concerned the yeast was in the brew, and the men who were to provide it must now be considered in more detail.

Thomas Brunner was one of a family of seven. His father, an Oxford lawyer and coroner, signed an agreement with the New Zealand Company for Thomas to serve for three years as an "improver" on its survey staff. His annual salary of £91/5s. plus rations began when he arrived in Nelson in October 1841. He was twenty years old. His status as improver gave him work at low wages to improve his skills, and after the usual grind of laying out sections and road-lines he became a second-class assistant surveyor. In August 1843 the diary of a Nelson politician and artist had this revealing entry: "Mr Tuckett informed us that one of the surveyors named Brunner had returned and said he had intelligence of an immense plain, in the interior, boundless to the eye, where there were birds larger than geese which killed their dogs, and to which the former inhabitants had escaped from the attacks of Raupero [Rauparaha]. Mr Tuckett said that he had sent Mr Brunner back with the promise that if he discovered it, it should be called the Brunner Plain. . . Mr Brunner had said that in former attempts to explore, the natives had misled us and taken us to the left, while this lay to the right, and that he himself had been further than the true road."

What of the Maoris in the South Island? We have seen that they were the essential guides of the North. But in the South?

Before the Pakeha and even in the South Island there were some routes where Maori enterprise and Maori courage had been the first to conquer the distances and the solitude. The mountains were not empty of bird life. Above the snow, the skirls of the kea raised echoes. In the bush the choruses of the bellbird and tui, the whirr of the berry-bellied pigeon, and the night cries of the kakapo, kiwi and weka were but routine. The skylines were stark in their grandeur. Snow ebbed and flowed according to sea-son, but over the higher ranges there was perpetual ice. Many of the rock ridges were broken, as though they were designed for teeth in a saw. Some precipices were made as though to terrify intruders. The breaks in these ranges formed natural saddles or passes, where strong and resolute men could cross from one valley to another valley. Do not talk of provinces, for the times that you must contemplate are before the Pakeha, when a riverbed was a road and a flax sandal made the imprint in the sand on river beaches.

The history of the passes that were probably used as keys to Maori trails in the Southern Alps will be recorded in following pages. For the moment we are in the top end of the South Island, where the stimulus to bush and mountain travel was war, or flight from war. The old-time Maori warrior needed speed on foot and knowledge of country that enabled him to outflank or surprise his enemies.[1] He had to know the arts of living off the land. His natural training as guerilla leader or commando officer excelled any-thing that he would now learn in an army school of bush and mountain warfare.

Living off the land was indeed a technical skill. For a party to prepare for a transalpine trail meant the gathering of wekas packed in kelp bags. Dried eels and whitebait would be useful to add to eels caught on the journey. Berries of totara and kahikatea would give variety to roots of the fern katoke. Dried mamaku (black-ribbed ponga) was another staple diet. These dried foods would be soaked overnight and then roasted or pounded between stones. Six men would start their trip with a hundredweight of food. If the party was large, the chief would only carry weapons, and slaves would take the mats and food. Women also could take heavy loads. The Pakeha mountaineer of today would be no better served by modern dehydrated foods or his somewhat unre-liable airdrops of supplies. The rough trails were hard on footwear, and the Maoris wore sandals that they refashioned from flax or mountain grass as they wore out.

Friction from dry sticks gave fire for cooking. Live birds such as pigeons, tuis, and wekas could be captured by traditional means. Gulls' eggs could be added to shellfish from the unpolluted sea. Flax ropes were used for tricky cliffs or river bluffs. The rivers themselves were crossed on rafts (mokihi) of wood or raupo, and weather forecasting was made possible by a study of clouds and twinkling stars.

To understand the achievements of Thomas Brunner it is necessary to know about the feats and fortitude of his guide, Kehu. In early accounts he features as Ekehu, but the E is merely the vocative E and therefore ornamental. We know from a sketch by Heaphy that Kehu was magnificently built, and from Brunner that he was a prince of bushmen. He

[1] The first crossing of the Haast Pass by Te Puoho in 1836 will be described later in its context.

would have accompanied Brunner on the trip of August 1843, for a receipt in National Archives shows that he was paid £2 for three weeks' wages. Heaphy not only gave us a fine sketch of the man Kehu but his pen portrait of his character must be quoted in full: "E Kehu, our guide, is thus a perfect bushman, and is of very great service on an expedition; he has none of the sluggishness of disposition so common to the Maori, but is active and energetic, displaying far more of the characteristics of the Indian savage than are to be seen in the usual lazy inhabitants of a pa; thoroughly acquainted with the 'bush', he appears to have an instinctive sense, beyond our comprehension, which enables him to find his way through the forest when neither sun nor distant object is visible, amidst gullies, brakes, and ravines in confused disorder, still onward he goes, following the same bearing, or diverging from it but so much as is necessary for the avoidance of impediments, until at length he points out to you the notch in some tree or the foot-print in the moss, which assures you that he has fallen upon a track, although one which he had not been previously acquainted with. A good shot, one who takes care never to miss his bird, a a capital manager of a canoe, a sure snarer of wild-fowl, and a superb fellow at a ford, is the same E Kehu; and he is worth his weight in tobacco!"

In tracing the history of exploration the most difficult thing for the modern reader to understand is that although an ordered and even civilised life could go on for settlers, the country beyond the ranges was regarded as being hostile as well as being unknown. A traveller who could write of the South Island thus could be doubly damned for ignorance as well as for lack of guts: "The greater portion of the western half appears to be a densely-timbered Alpine wilderness — a 'Black Forest', unfit for man or domestic beaste [sic]". Thomas Arnold has a better pen and a nobler vision when in the late 1840s he described Nelson so well: "Standing on Fort Hill in the middle of the town, and looking westward, one saw a range of mountains stretching for twenty miles or more. . . . Through gaps in this range could be seen higher peaks beyond, usually capped with snow . . . I have seen panoramas more beautiful, strictly speaking, than this — but never one more humanly delightful and enchanting, when the softness and delicacy of the air, the availableness of much of the land in view for human needs, and the vastness of the area of vision, are all taken into consideration."

How could Brunner and his surveying explorers contain themselves in this picturesque lotus-land of Nelson? Fortunately they had the curiosity, as well as the courage, as well as the economic necessity of

Thomas Brunner in middle age.

Charles Heaphy, V.C., in his military uniform.

54

The Mount Arthur Ranges in the distance from near Nelson. Heaphy painted this in 1841.

needing land for settlement and farming. Thus in 1843, the year when J. C. Fremont found the Great Salt Lake of North America and Castelnau had crossed South America through Brazil and Bolivia to the Pacific coast at Lima, Charles Heaphy, who had explored the Riwaka, and whose employment as draughtsman had not inhibited him from helping Captain Wakefield in searching for a good site for the settlement of Nelson, came back to Nelson in full vigour. He knew that however accurate were the charts of the coastline, the interior was virtually unknown. Further, he had a mind of his own, and thought that the country south-west of Lake Rotoiti must be investigated. He would explore, preferably with the approval of the New Zealand Company, but in any case, he would explore. In the event the Company authorised a maximum of £100 for the expedition, which included J. S. Spooner and three others. This figure was in fact a record high one for exploration in Nelson. The party found the grassy valley of the upper Buller (the Maori Kawatiri), met another survey party under Boys, sent by Tuckett, and followed the river down to the gorge — the Devil's Grip. From a climb above the gorge they could see that there was no large grassy plain to the south-west. They joined with the other survey party and trekked back to Nelson. Heaphy then returned to the Riwaka-Takaka country, followed coastlines in Golden Bay, and reported on his "most difficult journeying".

He made a trip to the Croiselles Harbour and Pelorus Sound in 1844. That same year J. C. Drake with two other men and a Maori followed earlier sorties from Nelson up the Maitai to cross to Pelorus, follow the Kaitauna valley, and camp close to the Wairau. The route was better, but the land was still the same area as before.

In 1845 the determined Charles Heaphy decided to push over the ranges and through the gorges to the level coastland said to be below Cape Foulweather [Foulwind]. Because the Buller was flooded it was difficult to live off the land. They followed Cotterell's trail up the Travers river, source of Lake Rotoiti, and climbed a peak to the east; the Nelson paper reported "Below, to the eastward diverged the various shoulders of the mountain and below them a slope of apparently fine land with patches of forest, extended to the sea, the very distant horizon of which was blended with the sky." This incursion into the Rainbow watershed of the Wairau had the usual undertone of short rations and the overtone of confused topography.

Now come three major journeys in which Thomas

Pelorus Sound; another barrier to explorers on foot.

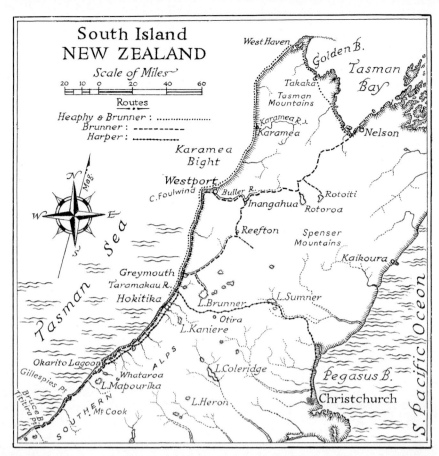

South Island
NEW ZEALAND
Scale of Miles
20 10 0 20 40 60
Routes
Heaphy & Brunner : ....
Brunner : ----------
Harper : ━━━━━━━

Sir William Fox, painter, explorer, premier.

Brunner features with stalwart Kehu in attendance and often in the lead. The first journey was early in 1846. Brunner, Heaphy and Kehu have already been described. To this trio of talent add William Fox, like Heaphy an artist; a future premier of New Zealand; ten years older than Heaphy; an agent for the New Zealand Company. Horses took loads from the Waimea to the Motupiko. When the four entered Heaphy's "big wood" they carried 75 lbs each. Provisions accounted for most of the burden: 2 cwt. of flour; 24 lbs of sugar, with tea and coffee; 20 lbs of ham; half a bottle of whisky (medicinal!). A double-barrelled gun and powder, a tin saucepan, an axe, a small tent, clothing and blankets comprised the rest of the party's gear. Heaphy's lively account describes the party as including ". . . a good plain cook, a first-class tailor, two glee singers, and a dispensing physician".

He refers to one of the party's appearance: "...with his immense burden, forcibly reminded one of a grotesque Atlas", and another " . . . with his small body and topping load, suggested the idea of an over-grown and peripatetic mushroom". The account of the travelling is reminiscent of missionary endeavours in the north: ". . . of the most laborious kind to a person heavily laden, as, although almost free from underbrush, the ground is covered with wet moss . . . and the path is frequently impeded by dead timber and thorny brambles".

At Lake Rotoiti they found the Buller fordable and Kehu took them to the Howard river where they saw

58

the remains of bark huts built by Maoris hunting the kiwi and the kakapo. They made a cache of food ratproof by burying it with walls of bark covered by ashes. Kehu took a route that climbed high above the gorges and encouraged his Pakehas by mimicry of panting, stooping under a load, and falling as though exhausted. On 11 February they saw Lake Rotoroa far below and descended to it. Kehu here located a small canoe which took them down the lake to the Gowan. Kehu caught eels in plenty, ". . . chanting his Wesleyan missionary service, mixing with the translated version of the ritual special incantations to the taipo [devil] of the lake and river for propitious weather and easy fords." In the morning there were ". . . four fine eels roasting for our breakfast, and another four were hanging from an adjacent tree".

Another day they explored the lake in the canoe, surprising wild birds, admiring the Spenser Mountains, eating pigeon and damper and discussing the future of this beautiful lake as a tourist resort. They made a great haul of pigeons, blue ducks, eels and wekas.

Heaphy found the method of snaring wekas "singular and amusing": "The native, when in a locality which he thinks likely to be frequently by woodhens, imitates, with a whistle made of a flax-leaf, the cry of the bird. . . . If one be within hearing it will answer, or more generally several will respond to the cry, and the native, listening for a moment attentively, informs you of their number and position. . . . When at leisure, the Maori provides himself with two slight sticks or canes, of the lengths of about four and six feet. To the end of the shorter he attaches a bunch of feathers, or even leaves, and to the longer a running noose of flax, and with these proceeds in the direction whence the sound came. When he considers himself near enough he stops, and crouching down amongst the underwood, but without caring to be concealed, imitates the more familiar call of the bird by a peculiar grunting sound made in the throat. In a short time the woodhen appears, and the native rustles the feathers at the end of the stick, making a chirping noise in unison, and the weka, mistaking the moving object for a bird, is led by the pugnacity of its dispo-

Fox painted this scene of calm landscape in the Matakitaki (Aglionby) valley, at the head of the Buller. Kehu provides the action by snaring a weka. The work is dated 20 February 1846.

sition to attack it, in advancing to do which the noose is quietly put over its head, and with a jerk upwards is caught alive."

A characteristic entry of Heaphy's dealt with the erection of a blanket house, with walls of bark: "Amused ourselves with the pursuit of comfort under difficulties."

Swagging over a low pass led to the Tiraumea valley, which included open country. By 18 February they reached the Buller ("singular and remarkable") and found its gorge in one place was ". . . amid high and uncouthly-shaped masses and piles of rock, divided as if by some earthquake force, and worn smooth by the mighty and ceaseless action of the river".

Heaphy admired Kehu's skill when the Buller had to be forded. The most difficult part was in the centre where ". . . it rushed with impetuosity in a deep, hollow wave to its greater velocity below the ford, where it became a race crested with a high and broken ripple." Kehu led the crossing. He ". . . made one of his comical grimaces, and entered the stream,

the depth of which now became apparent, and ere he had reached the centre of the river the water was up to his waist. One or two of the party now ran down the side of the river, in order to be able to afford assistance should he be carried down; but with once or twice staggering when exposed to the greatest pressure, and a spring downward with the current as he neared the further bank, he reached the opposite side in safety, not forgetting to evince his contempt for the river and exultation at having crossed, in a series of grotesque gesticulations and vehement abuse of the river and all its tributaries."

Fox was not so lucky or so skilful. He was swept off his feet in spite of a pole he carried to help him balance in the current, but was a good enough swimmer to make the far bank. Brunner found a wider ford and Heaphy swam at another place.

Below the gorges there was a fine stretch of river flats in the Buller: the Matukituki of the Maoris and Aglionby of Heaphy.

By this time the party was near the Maruia junction. They solemnly believed they were only twenty

Another 1846 painting by Fox of the exploring party. The men are wading the Buller River.

miles from the coast, but lacked enough food to continue the journey to the Buller mouth. Kehu guided them back across what is now the main highway route over the pass and known to thousands of motorists as the Hope Saddle. The journey had been fertile in providing paintings. The experience in incessant river wading was to prove useful to Brunner later. The trip ended on 1 March with Heaphy's laconic entry: "Walked into Nelson".

No sooner were Brunner and Heaphy back than they were all set for another expedition. Fox finished his despatch of 12 March with "I have persuaded Mr Brunner who is a very zealous explorer to undertake a journey down the coast to Cape Farewell to the mouth of the Buller river . . . under the guidance of the native [who] accompanied us." Kehu was certainly a regular for mentions in despatches. The objective, the Buller mouth, was doubly important: it would link the explorers as though from the upper reaches; it would amplify reports of 1844 from Thomas, a sealer, who had been attracted by Maori reports of flat and fertile land and who had actually crossed the bar. Furthermore, Thomas had also reported that a Maori message on a board in the sand had directed (in Maori) other travellers to follow the writer to Cape Farewell. Clearly this meant the coast could be followed, even above its cliffs.

When on 17 March the party left Nelson the three men hoped to take their exploration to the Arahura valley with its source of greenstone. They reached Golden Bay by boat, crossed from the Aorere (near the present Collingwood township) and reached the Pakawau Inlet with loads of 80 lbs composed of flour and other provisions, powder, shot, instruments, books and boots. Heaphy walked to Cape Farewell and theorised about its formation. He was responsive to the weather: "As I stood upon the cape, a furious squall of rain and hail was driving past. . . . The mist obscured the view for more than a quarter of a mile around, while the noise of the dash of the breakers on the cliff below roared away in concert with the thunder. And the storm for the time seemed universal."

At West Wanganui there was some unpleasantness with the chief Niho, an ally of Te Rauparaha, who tried to block the Pakehas from heading southwards. Niho had a supporter who was said to have talked three prisoners to death. Brunner and Heaphy refused to bribe Niho with money but pacified him with four sticks of tobacco. They had engaged another local Maori as porter: Etau, who could carry a huge load and snare wekas but "his intellect was not the highest".

The coastal journey was sometimes held up by rain and high tides. Fording rivers was a problem. It was a toss-up at one place whether to use a flax-stalk raft or a deep ford. Small rock caves could be augmented as shelters by a house of nikau palm leaves. Pauas, sea eggs, and sea anemones helped eke out the food. Heaphy noted that the sea egg, "though very palatable, would be much improved by vinegar and condiments". He thought the sea anemones "not a favourite food of Scotch terrier dogs". Other times the route lay up steep and dangerous cliffs with rotten native-made ropes rangling as though in threat. He gave dramatic asides about the coolness and alacrity needed to leap from rock to rock at the base of cliffs or to worm around ledges under overhanging rocks.

The party passed a former sealing reef and station. They were impressed by the beautiful valley of the Whakapoai, now mapped as the Heaphy. By 20 April they reached the Karamea river. To cross this they had to make a raft, twenty-two feet by five inches, and capable of taking a load of men and packs of 700 lbs: "It floated with its upper surface about an inch above the water. It was sufficiently strong to rise over a considerable swell without working loose, and might be paddled at the rate of about two miles an hour." Because the flax absorbed water "it was necessary to throw overboard the dog". This was Rover, who apparently did not like the taste of sea anemones. Heaphy himself had to abandon the craft to allow it to keep the provisions and the clothes dry.

Talking of provisions, Heaphy wrote that they had shrunk to 10 lbs of flour, 2 lbs of pork, and a few ounces of tea and sugar "laid up as a resource only to be used in cases of extreme want or illness". Dinner one night was cabbage palm stem and mussels. The following day the rations were half a weka each.

The Mohikinui river was a tough crossing: "Here, joining our several sticks together in place of a pole, and holding them horizontally before us, we entered the river together abreast, going at once into the deep part of the stream." On 27 April a Maori, Aperahama (Abraham), appeared with his son and daughter. He had never seen a Pakeha before. Heaphy found him ". . . an exceedingly intelligent native, and perhaps the finest specimen of the Maori that could be found in the island". He gave the exploring party some of his food and news from the south. Nearly two months later Aperahama arrived in Nelson with a note from Heaphy about the progress and the difficulties of the expedition.

The Kawatiri (Buller) was in a flood when they arrived on its bank on 30 April. The Maoris repaired a piece of old canoe by adding flax-stalks and leaves and a layer of earth. As non-swimmer, Etau paddled the contraption across the Buller. Kehu made other

The dog Rover, Thomas Brunner, and the ladder of rata vine on the Miko Cliff, sketched by Heaphy.

trips and one by one the Pakehas reached safety. On 3 May Heaphy referred to "the long range of snowy mountains, which Cook denominated 'The Southern Alps' " and noted that "they appear like ice islands lying off the coast".

The narrative mentioned rain and wind, "hot penguin soup, which would be a capital mess were it not so fishy", other Maoris met in isolated settlements, the recital by Kehu and company of litanies, psalms, creeds and the marriage service (exercises of entertainment rather than of religious zeal), and ". . . birds, fortunately, still plentiful, and cooking our chief amusement". Winter hail and rain arrived. Slowly the party progressed. Heaphy noted detached coal in a riverbed.

Some of the obstacles were truly spectacular. Here is an account of the Miko cliff: "It is 120 feet in height, and its descent was first effected by a war party, the natives composing which let down a ladder made of the rata vine of the forest above. There are now two stages of ladders, made of short pieces of the ropy rata, lashed together with flax, with steps at irregular distance, the whole very shaky and rotten . . . our baggage and the dog had to be hoisted up by a flax rope." The route lay past Punakaiki, and so to the site of Greymouth, where the river was crossed in a canoe on 25 May.

The Taramakau pa was occupied by Ngaitahu refugees from tribal wars. They were very hospitable to the strangers, and fed them on winter supplies of potatoes, eels, whitebait, leeks, sprats and taro. At the Arahura they rested. This was their southernmost point. Heaphy made some very significant observations, such as ". . . the mountain chain commences . . . its highest peak is the mountain Te Hauraki

The Taramakau Pa was in reality at the mouth of the Arahura River. The top strip of the sketch by Heaphy shows the Southern Alps culminating in Mount Cook, the "Te Hauraki" (Aorangi) of the explorers. The pa is shown in the bottom strip.

62

[Aorangi], which the natives assert is of the greatest elevation of any in the island." His reference to Maori reports of a route up the Taramakau to a pass to Port Cooper (Lyttelton) was a key to Brunner's subsequent exploration and objectives. He also noted that the Arahura was the home of the much-prized greenstone. Heaphy also mapped the coastline as he traversed it. This was truly professional exploring.

The return trip had the handicaps of bad weather, fever, poor food, and general weakness. Still, they had to climb up and down and across their cliffs, to push through the scrub, to tackle every new river ford as though it was their last — as well it could be if they grew careless and were drowned. A crossing of the Buller on a driftwood raft took twenty anxious minutes. The worst part of the Mohikinui ford was the carrying of heavy logs to the water's edge. At the mouth of the Heaphy the diary entry read: "We were now in about as low condition as it was possible to be still to retain health. Lying for three or four days together in a small hut during heavy rains, or when waiting for the subsidence of a river, was perhaps more weakening in effect than was the absence of nutritious food. . . Four miles a day, including stoppages for rain, was the most we could average."

On 18 August they reached Nelson, after being away for five hard months. A few months later, Brunner and Kehu were all set for their greatest journey of all. Heaphy's career lay in varied fields: art; surveying; bush warfare; member of Parliament; judge of the Maori Land Court. His VC was the only one awarded to a Colonist soldier in the Maori Wars, gained after persistent assertions that he had earned it.

It is interesting to reflect that the West Coast between West Wanganui and Karamea is still virtually unroaded and untracked. The scrub is still fierce though admitting of trails for goats and deer. The cliffs are still steep and crumbly, but there are no frayed flax ropes left by itinerant Maoris to guide travellers. Indeed it would be something of a novelty if a few young men of the 1970s were to repeat the traverse from Farewell Spit to the Arahura using the beaches and the cliffs. From Karamea and south there is today a magnificently scenic series of roads; the rivers are all bridged; solid food is never scarce.

Brunner was in no doubt about the extent or the complexity of his next expedition. He wanted a better knowledge of the interior, in particular the part of the Buller that he had not yet traversed. He wanted to follow the West Coast as far down as Milford

Kehu snaring a weka at the Arahura Pa. Mount Cook is on the skyline.

Sound, if that was possible. He wanted to prove and cross a pass from the West Coast to Canterbury or Otago. William Fox was sympathetic to the journey, Kehu was available, a friend of his, Pikewate, was added to the party, and — unfortunately in some ways — the wives of the guides insisted on going with Brunner. The great journey cost £36 18s 4d. For the natives Brunner bought boots, "trowsers", shirts, belts, a blanket, caps, shoes, calico, mending materials at a cost of £8 0s 6d. For himself he bought two pairs of boots, three pairs of "trowsers", a strap and shirts, four pairs of socks, two blankets and a shooting coat at a cost of £8 14s. The provisions and necessaries were two guns, shot-belt and flask; 16 lbs tobacco, 1 cwt flour; powder and shot; salt, pepper, a box of caps; biscuits, tea, sugar, matches; cooking-pot, knives and tomahawk; and other small articles, all at a cost of £20 3s 10d.

The journey began on 4 December 1846. Mule and canoe transport helped the first two weeks. The energetic Brunner climbed a hill above Lakes Rotoiti and Rotoroa to see what lay to the east ". . . but found it entirely shut out by the high snowy range". The disadvantages of taking wives was apparent on 2 January 1847: ". . . my two female companions quarrelled and fought. Their husbands taking part in the combat, I had much difficulty in reconciling them, and persuading them to continue their journey." Fording the Buller as they slowly descended its flats and gorges was always a problem. Kehu usually made a trial crossing. "We then agreed to venture, all five holding our stick, taking off all our clothes, and securing our loads high on our shoulders: the river in some places ran just mouth high, with a powerful current. We however reached the other side, having well wetted our clothes and loads." Fresh-water herrings, cabbage-tree roots, fern roots, and twelve hours of baking gave the party a good feed ". . . but rather too sweet for a diet".

The progress down valley was dot-and-carry-one. At one place they would stop for a week to accumulate and prepare provisions for the next stage. At another they would decide that incessant rain had spoilt everything and that they must return to a better place to do their cooking and to make a raft. Thus on 18 February they were again leaving their hut in an attempt to make better progress back down river. More often than not there were forced bivouacs to be endured: ". . . and just before dusk reached a large *ana,* or hole in the rocks, where we put up

In some places the Buller Gorge was a wide river and bed as well as steep sides.

for the night. The rain soon began to fall so heavily, that we were all afraid of being drowned in our shelter before morning by the rising of the river."

They found that a small raft was useful. This could take all the clothes and provisions. The fastest swimmers towed the raft on a flax-line; the others pushed from behind. On 26 February Brunner wrote: "I am getting so sick of this exploring, the walking and the diet being both so bad, that were it not for the shame of the thing, I would return to the more comfortable quarters of the Riwaka valley." A few days later he noted that ". . . this is without exception the very worst country I have seen in New Zealand; not a bird to be had or seen; and the few fish there are in the river will not bite during rain or during a fresh." Thousands of sandflies, influenza, an inadequate diet of fern-root, and the difficult terrain made Brunner despair.

His diary entry of 21 March spoke volumes: "Rain continuing, dietary shorter, strength decreasing, spirits failing, prospects fearful." However they were close to the Inangahua country, edible fungus and eels gave some relief and, when they later reached better going, they were rewarded by wekas, kakas, teal and kakapos. In May life grew grim again: the final gorges of the Buller were tough; food was scarce. Consider this sad entry of 23 May: "Hunger again compelled us to shift our quarters in search of food, but finding none, I was compelled, though very reluctantly, to give my consent to killing my dog Rover. The flesh of a dog is very palatable, tasting something between mutton and pork. It is too richly flavoured to eat by itself." [1]

Bluffs and gorges gave way to dense bush and undergrowth with the routine refinement of supplejacks, prickly lawyer vines, rotten logs and mud. On the last day of May they heard the roar of the tide," which was to me as good as a dinner," Brunner noted.

The potato gardens were empty so the explorers filled their bellies with seaweed: "So much for hunger." This was the site of the future Westport. They crossed the Buller in a canoe, and were welcomed by three Maori families who gave them mussels and fern-root. The four months travelling down the Buller had weakened the party for the gruelling trek from the Buller to the Grey. By 1 July they were back at the Grey and the Taramakau, feasting on plenty of potatoes. Brunner speculated about the identity of "Kai Mataiu", "a lofty-capped

mountain", probably Mt Rolleston.

Brunner telescoped his journal for the next three months into notes of Maori customs, appreciation of their generous help with food, dismay that the wild dogs had "almost extirpated" wekas, kakapos and kiwis, and topographical notes about Lake Ellesmere in Canterbury. On 12 October he left for the south with local Maoris. There was no Highway Six to the Haast, no wayside pubs and farms. There were the sands and the shingle, the swamps, the bluffs, the bush, and, above all, the rivers.

He swam rivers, crossed one in a canoe, forded another chin-deep, made sketches that never survived, and sometimes made an entry as imperishable as the following: "I believe I have now acquired the two greatest requisites for bushmen in New Zealand, viz. the capability of walking barefoot, and the proper method of cooking and eating fern root. I had often looked forward with dread to the time when my shoes would be worn out, often fearing I should be left a barefooted cripple in some desolate black birch forest, on this deserted coast; but now I can trudge along merrily barefoot, or with a pair of native sandals, called by the natives pairairai, made of the leaves of the flax, or, what is more durable, the leaves of the ti or flax tree. I can make a sure footing in crossing rivers, and ascending or descending precipices; in fact, I feel I am just beginning to make exploring easy work."

He found Okarito when the rata began to bloom "one of the most beautiful pieces of scenery I have seen in New Zealand". At Tititira Head, below Paringa, he crushed his foot and strained an ankle. This was his southernmost point and he had to rest. On 11 December he left Paringa "once more to see the face of a white man, and hear my native tongue". Back at the Grey he enjoyed the varied food of bush fruit, flax honey, eels, potatoes and turnips. Sandflies abounded, and smoke from fires was the only protection.

Late in January 1848 Brunner canoed up the Grey, found the coalfield later named after him, visited the lake also graced by his name and, if he had but realised it, trod part of a future railway route. Near the present site of Reefton he climbed a mountain from which he glimpsed high-country tussock beyond the Lewis Pass. Although he wished to take this way over to Canterbury his guides insisted on returning to Nelson via the Buller. So on 23 March it was back to the Buller, with bad weather, the colds of winter, semi-starvation, and a temporary paralysis. Faithful Kehu encouraged him. He lost his sketches in a fire. On 15 June he was back at Motueka run where the farmer gave him "a hearty

---

[1] Rover was later mourned by his owner, a Scotchman, who told Captain Stokes of the *Acheron* of the dog's sagacity. See Nancy M. Taylor's scholarly editing of Brunner's journal.

The rugged line of the West Coast at a point beyond Brunner's farthest South at Tititira Head, Paringa.

The Okarito Bluff, characteristic of the West Coast. These men of the nineties are carrying big swags.

welcome, and the luxury of a taste of good tobacco". He wrote: "So, thank God, I am once more among civilized men." He had been away for 550 days, and felt astonished that he could both understand and speak English as well as ever. He paid this tribute to Kehu: "I found my native Ekehu of much use. . . to Ekehu I owe my life — he is a valuable and attached servant." Brunner went on to carry out other survey work in Nelson.

He was honoured by the Royal Geographical Society in London, and in New Zealand by subsequent generations who venerate him as one of the greatest, perhaps the greatest explorer. He died in 1874 at fifty-three years.

In fact Brunner did not do well as head of the Nelson Survey Department. With lack of staff and funds some of the surveys were skimped, and Brunner did not fight vigorously. It may be that the theory that his privations had undermined his health and accounted for his relatively early death could also explain his seeming acquiescence at the state of the Nelson survey.

Men such as Brunner did not reap the material rewards of the successful goldminers and pastoralists, but their brave survey work made it possible for other pioneers to prosper where earlier travellers had nearly starved or drowned.

After the tangled wilderness of the West Coast, the quest of sheepmen for new country in Marlborough is less dramatic. Instead of the rainforest there were the wide expanses where waving tussocks devoured the miles and the shingle threatened the riverflats. Rivers were still a danger, the more so because they appeared to be harmless. Enterprise and determination were needed to back up hunger for new land or new routes. The main valleys in this contrasting scenery are now well marked by main roads, red woolsheds, and pleasant homesteads nestling in belts of exotic trees. Aircraft fly in a few minutes over ranges that took men days of danger to cross. But, off the beaten track, conditions of travel are not so vastly different from those of the 1860s. This must be said: tramping and climbing parties of today meet some of the experiences faced

An aerial view of the Buller River. The bushed ridges seem as though to interlock.

Tapuaenuku, the highest peak of the Inland Kaikoura Range and the Clarence valley as seen from Mount Kaitarau of the Seaward Kaikouras. Mounts Mitre and Alarm lie to the left of Tapuaenuku.

by pioneer stockmen a hundred years ago.

Towards the end of 1848 Brunner examined all the known passes between Nelson and the Wairau and sought further ones. With Kehu and another Maori, and an amateur surveyor, the party weaved in and out the Maitai, over the Dun Mountain and into the Pelorus, where they had the familiar experiences of heavy rain, flooded camps, improvising a flax raft, and dysentery. They returned to Nelson by other variants of Wairau topography. Four days later Brunner and Kehu tried two other passes.

The scene moved to country south of the Wairau. The men too changed. Brunner presumably was not well enough to push hard towards Canterbury. Lieutenant-Governor Eyre, who has entered the pages of this book earlier (see page 31) now sounds an energetic blast. He made the first ascent, or nearly so, of the highest peak of the Inland Kaikoura Range. 9471 feet. Recollect that the Alpine Club, London, was not even born at that date. Mountaineering, even in Switzerland, was sporadic. John Ruskin was travelling actively from Geneva and Chamonix, but he had only derision for climbers, whom he likened to animals on a greasy pole.

Eyre had a companion in W. J. W. Hamilton, Governor's private secretary and fellow-explorer with Captain J. L. Stokes of the *Acheron,* who had the latest knowledge of North Canterbury. Eyre also had his secretary, J. D. Ormond, and some Maoris. Ostensibly to find the Maori track from the Wairau to North Canterbury, Eyre and Hamilton went up the Awatere valley which ran parallel to the Wairau. Eyre decided to climb Tapuaenuku to spy out the proposed route to Canterbury. At the snowline Hamilton packed it in; the party had no proper mountain gear or survey gear, but Eyre had his innate determination strengthened by his experiences in the lonely deserts of Australia. Eyre, Ormond and some Maoris reached the near summit of the mountain. Here there was no Grey breathing down his neck to wreck his alpine programme as had happened with Tongariro.

Eyre's account was: "The closing in of night and the appearance of a strong breeze setting in compelled me to endeavour to obtain a halting place and shelter for the night. . . I had succeeded in reaching about 300 yards in distance and about 50 feet in elevation from the very highest point — every difficulty had been overcome . . . one quarter of an hour more daylight would have enabled me to accomplish this [i.e. the very highest viewpoint], but late as it was and uncertain as to the weather I dare not keep my party on the summit for the night." They had their benightment at some 8,700 feet, the first such experience in the history of New Zealand mountaineering.

There was another first also: the first fatality, when Wiremu Hoeta slipped to his death in an inaccessible ravine. One wonders how Eyre would break this news to Grey? He did so in a matter-of-fact and topography-laden despatch dated 21 November 1849: "Sir I have the honour to inform your Excellency that I returned to Wellington, this morning from the Middle Island, after only a fortnight's absence in consequence of an accident having happened to one of the Natives of my Party — During this short excursion I have been enabled to examine a good deal of the country east of the Wairau, on the Awaterre (the Kaipara te hau district) as far as the highest of the snowy mountains commonly called 'Kaikouras' but known by the Native Name of 'Tapuaenuku'.

"This district is generally very grassy and well watered and is well suited for either Cattle or Sheep — there is however as on the Wairau a great scarcity of timber.

"From what I saw of the country there did not appear to me to be any great difficulty in the way of croping between Wairau and the Port Cooper country — the best line for which is up the 'Wairau' and 'Waiopai' rivers passing behind or on the island side of the great Snowy mountain Tapuaenuku.

"I must regret that the unfortunate occurrence to which I have alluded in the earlier part of this despatch, necessitated me to give up my intended attempt to connect the Wairau with the Port Cooper country.

"As far as I could see the country to be 'passed thru' tho' somewhat broken and hilly was apparently grassy and quite free from timber — further to the South-west there might probably have been one or two belts of fresh to crop but I do not think these could either be extensive or difficult."

The obstacles of mountain ranges must have been impressive to Nelson surveyors as to other settlers. J. W. Barnicoat of Nelson in 1842 had observed ". . . this country beats Cornwall in hilliness. . . there are five hills to one at home." But he was writing about Wellington and not Nelson. The mountains such as Tapuaenuku must have seemed tremendous

to men seeking trails from Marlborough to the south.

Nelson was more than anxious to offload some of its surplus stock on Canterbury. Squatters and other sheepmen were able to explore or to stock country in the absence of detailed maps and knowledge. In 1850 three parties were active. Lieutenant A. Impey of the Indian Army went up the Awatere with a sheepman, a whaler and two Maoris, but retreated in face of heavy rain, snow, dysentery and general puzzlement about the topography.

The next shot was better, by Captain W. M. Mitchell, another Indian Army man, Captain Edwin H. Dashwood, and an old whaler, Harris. Mitchell had already seen the head of the Awatere from some 6,000 feet when he had climbed from the head of the Waihopai branch of the Wairau. The expedition left in April 1850 with a mare and a mule. Winter greeted them. Matagouri was the only firewood in this valley, which they named after HMS *Acheron*.

After somewhat amphibious travelling through a gorge they saw the country we now know as Molesworth. Mitchell thought prophetically but by accident that the grazing would be better for cattle than for sheep, a fact that generations of sheepmen later ignored. They lived on wekas caught by the dog.

At the Clarence valley Mitchell noted traces of Maori travel, but it is likely that these were made by J. S. Caverhill, an exploring runholder from Canterbury. Although Mitchell lost his only compass in a river ford he kept his sense of direction, and led his party over another range to Hanmer, thence to the Waiau, the coast near Cheviot and a meeting with Caverhill at Motunau. The value of the Mitchell Dashwood route was not great in itself but it was a beginning.

Late in 1850 the squatter F. A. Weld, a future premier of New Zealand, used the head of the Awatere to reach the Acheron via the Guide river but he mistook the Clarence for the Waiau. On the strength (or rather the weakness) of this, Alphonse Clifford, a young brother of his partner Charles Clifford, with three musterers took 700 wethers over Barefell Pass, but the difficulties of travelling down the wrong river proved too much and the flock had to be abandoned.

At the end of the following year E. J. Lee improved on the Mitchell-Dashwood route and rode a horse right through to Christchurch. He linked up with Edward Jollie and took 1,800 sheep from the Awatere to Cheviot. Jollie had met Mitchell and Dashwood at the end of their 1850 journey: "I happened to be in Cass's house at Riccarton with Captain Thomas when two very rough dirty-looking men with packs on their

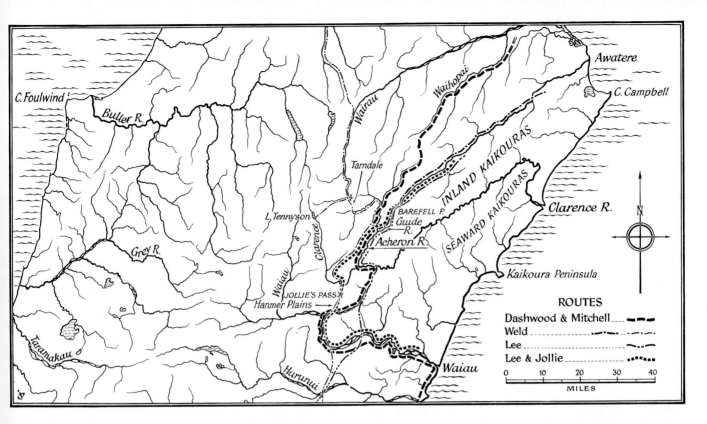

backs arrived at the door, with was open. Thomas who was taken by surprise at their appearance, immediately shouted out, 'Who the devil are you?' to which they meekly replied they were from Nelson overland. As they spoke like gentlemen they were at once welcomed and supplied with a glass of grog each."

Jollie described his pass from the Clarence to Hanmer thus: ". . . arrived at a point whence I could see through an opening in the Snowy Hills, the yellow grassy hills beyond the Hanmer Plain". Because of matagouri and spaniards they had to take the sheep by a high-level route and then burn the Jollies Pass scrub prior to taking the sheep through.

Sheep in the Clarence valley near Jollie's Pass.

In March 1855 Weld retrieved his reputation as an explorer. With Alphonso Clifford he left Tophouse and penetrated the Wairau-Rainbow flat: "The two rivers . . . flowed out of a formidable barrier of mountains in our front, whose rocky peaks rose darkly above us, patched here and there, in spite of the long-continued summer's heat, with dazzling dots of snow." They discovered the inland grass of Tarndale, Island Pass and Lake Tennyson. This was the view of Tarndale from a ridge: "Light mists floating about the summit slightly impeded our view, yet did not from an altitude of nearly 7,000 feet above sea level prevent us from ascertaining that the inland grass country lay below us. . . .

"Immediately on our left, the southeast branch of the Wairau flowed out of a rock-bound gorge, whilst to our right little was visible but craggy and snow-patched mountains, in which the valley of the west Wairau seemed soon to break and lose itself."

Weld gave a clear description of Lake Tennyson at the head of the Clarence: "It lies in an ampitheatre of lofty peaks, bold in outline, dark in colour, except where brightened by sunlight and relieved by patches of snow scattered in clefts of the rock." It is only fair to add that all these routes admitted of horses or mules being taken as pack animals, in contrast to the heavy swagging endured by parties further west or south.

Tarndale and the Island Pass from the upper Clarence.

Lake Tennyson, discovered in 1855 by F. A. Weld.

The Gouland Downs is a very important link for the Heaphy track and would be traversed by any new road between Karamea and Collingwood.

Weld finally went out to Jollies Pass via the Clarence. The Nelson provincial government now knew that the Canterbury runs could be stocked from Nelson by an inland trail. There were still other corners of Nelson to be explored. The legendary plains of the Maoris were still as elusive as ever. Although a map of 1850 shows the Heaphy (Wakapohai) and Aorere rivers in their correct place it is likely that their first physical examination was made late in 1856 by James Mackay and John Clark. A Mr Gouland had later applied for this area of "rushes and mosses" which accounts for the name Gouland Downs being given to the area which lies between the Heaphy and the Aorere. Mackay eventually pioneered the route from Karamea to Collingwood now known as the Heaphy Track, though Charles Heaphy never traversed inland on that route. John Rochfort and Frank Flowers also explored in this country. Today there is a call from tourist and local interests to take a road from Karamea to Collingwood, to make a round trip comparable to the Haast Pass but not as scenically magnificent or difficult to construct.

72

Another route became important: the Lewis Pass
from the Maruia branch of the Buller to the Lewis
and Hope branches of the Waiau. A pipe-opener to
the Lewis Pass exploration was the work between the
Grey and Nelson by James Mackay, described as a
man of iron, who was followed later by Dr Haast.
In February 1860 W. T. L. Travers and C. Maling
complemented the activity of H. Lewis. Travers was
realistic when he wrote: "Travelling in the unexplored
regions of this country is by no means a romantic or
adventurous undertaking, but it is on the contrary a
very matter-of-fact business, involving considerable
labour with no small share of dirt and hard living."
Travers and Maling crossed the Lewis Pass from the
north, and thought the Lewis and Boyle rivers were
feeders of the Grey, i.e. flowing to the West Coast.

Later it was proved these rivers led to the Hope,
Waiau and the Hanmer Plains.

A New Zealand Historic Places Trust plaque sets
the exploration in perspective. The Lewis Pass has
for long been a key stock route and today it is yet
more significant: it carries a well-graded modern road
across the mountains. It is less spectacular than the
other transalpine roads over Arthur's Pass-Otira or
Lake Wanaka-Haast but as an all-weather road, it is
seldom vulnerable to heavy snow or dangerous slips.
Finally John Rochford discovered the nearby Amuri
Pass from the Grey to the Doubtful, and gained a
bonus from the Nelson Government. It was used for a
bridle track but could not compete in any way with
the Lewis Pass route.

Mt Gloriana and the Maruia valley from near the summit of the Lewis Pass.
The Cannibal Gorge lies below.

Invariably odd pockets remained to be investigated. Rochfort continued to do detailed mapping in the Wangapeka and other rough country. Geological surveyors entered the field, and needed other kinds of detail for their maps. As an example, though a late one, take James Mackintosh Bell of the Geological Survey, in 1908. He was a PhD and a traveller, as well as a geologist, and his journey concerned the north-west corner of Nelson. He was a good leader and he had a good party: Jack Clarke, an alpine guide who as a young man had taken part in the first ascent of Mt Cook in 1894, Professor Patrick Marshall, author of textbooks, and Jim Cadigan. The camp at the mouth of the Heaphy was well sited: "Before us lay the labyrinth of forest-covered mountains, among which the river lost itself in the blue haze to the eastward, while on our ears fell the unceasing roar of the waves as they pounded upon the stretch of sand beach southward."

In February the party left their base to examine the country between the mouth of the Heaphy and the Mt Arthur Tableland. They were forced by the topography of the Divide to take a zigzag course. They began their trip with food for four days, a decision that contributed to empty bellies as the days grew.

A tedious climb of 3,000 feet through bush and subalpine scrub led to the rolling grass of the Gunner Downs where they camped under beech trees and boulders of granite. Below them there spread far away to the horizon the blue stretches of the Tasman Sea. They bedded down cheerfully. Crossing the Gunner Downs next day a fog rolled over them at 9 a.m. and

The highest point of the Lewis Pass, 2,968 ft., where the highway levels out before traversing the Maruia valley.

An aerial view towards the rugged Aorere headwaters where Bell and his companions were light on food.

made them camp for that day. The third day out the weather was fine but limestone chasms forced the party over matted scrub too dense to scramble through. They camped by seepage-holes in moss. Bird song serenaded them.

At noon the next day a sawtooth ridge looked difficult. Food was running short, and they caught wekas and boiled them. Another day took them along the ridge but, alas, it led to the Roaring Lion branch of the Karamea and not to the Tableland. The evening was calm and peaceful: kiwis, wekas, kakapos called. Having no reserves of food they had to return back along the ridge and head for the Aorere river, thence to Collingwood.

The next day they ate their last two meals and covered the upper eight miles of the Aorere. They threw stones at wekas, boiled the birds, and kept the bones to suck on their starvation journey. Bell carried a dozen dried apricots as reserve. Cadigan begged for one: "If I could have but one of those," he said, "I

would be twice the man."

About the middle of the afternoon of the seventh day they reached the mouth of the Burgoo and found an old camp in ruins, but no food. At nightfall they trudged on, in such a state of fatigue and hunger that no one spoke. But Cadigan got another weka, and then they came on a clear broad pool beneath a waterfall. A mother and four half-grown grey mountain ducks floated serenely on the placid surface. Three ducklings were caught and made a grand feast. At last, on the following day, they reached their first habitation: a farm forty miles from the head of the river.

To the tramper or mountaineer or hunter of today the expedition seems to have been ill provided considering its objectives and the calibre of its members. But even though a few pounds of rice could have saved the hunger pangs, the trip was memorable in one way: it marked the re-entry of professional geologists into the field of exploration.

Canterbury and Westland

The scene was larger, the mountain decor grander, the search for grazing land later in Canterbury than in Marlborough. Westland was different again: land of rainforest and floods, red rata and blue-green glacier icefalls, gold, timber and coal. The hazards and barriers made a mockery of advance. In Canterbury a fit man could walk twenty miles in twelve hours. In Westland a gorge might take twelve hours for a mile. The men who explored these different places were mostly surveyors, sheepmen, gold diggers. The Main Divide of the Southern Alps that was the boundary between Canterbury and Westland gave passes to men who had some ability in mountain travel.

The Canterbury Plains from the Bridle Track between Lyttelton and Christchurch. This panorama by E. Norman shows the distant line of the outer ranges, often mistaken for the Southern Alps.

It is difficult for people of the 1970s to place themselves back in the time when Canterbury was unsettled and unexplored. Who can think of Christchurch as a place of flax and swamps, or the fertile plains as a mass of tussock with rank growth of matagouri and speargrass? Settlers burnt their way into the country; their bullock wagons forded the ferocious rivers.

A considerable Maori population lived in Canterbury before the advent of the Pakeha but the combination of civil wars from 1810 and raids by Te Rauparaha and his Ngatitoa warriors between 1830 and 1832 reduced a total of perhaps 3,500 to a seventh of that number. Whalers were the first white men to gain a toehold in Canterbury. They visited Banks Peninsula in 1835. Port Cooper (Lyttelton) and Akaroa had excellent harbours as bases for whaling.

A whaling captain, W. B. Rhodes, was so impressed by the land that in 1839 he took cattle to Akaroa, thereby establishing the first cattle station in the South Island. Agricultural farming began in 1840 with the arrival of James Herriot and McGillivray at Riccarton. This venture was abandoned, probably because the party could not get a proper title to the land. French settlement at Akaroa succeeded in 1838 but not French sovereignty. For the story of Canterbury exploration, move to Lyttelton and the Canterbury Plains. Captains E. Daniell and G. Duppa, with William Deans inspected the access in August 1841. Daniell wrote an enthusiastic report to the New Zealand Company: "A splendid district of flat land . . . covered with luxuriant vegetation."

Governor Hobson would not allow the New Zealand

Company settlers to proceed to Lyttelton because the French land claims were pending for Banks Peninsula. The New Zealand Company settled for Nelson. Hobson had another reason for his opposition to settlement in Canterbury: it took settlers far from the reach of his Government at Auckland and he did not want to move to Port Nicholson (Wellington). William Deans returned in 1842 so impressed by the farming potential that he prepared to leave Wellington for good. He was of course too busy with his new location to have time to explore beyond its boundaries of swamp and bush.

While it was true that in 1831 a flax-trader, Joseph Price, and a trading master of a barque had walked from Lyttelton to Kaiapoi they left no account other than a record that the entrance to the Waimakariri river could not be crossed even with a Maori pilot. The first real journey was made by William Heaphy who was, like his namesake Charles, a surveyor's assistant in the New Zealand Company employ. When his party in Otago was recalled to Wellington he decided to walk north. He reached the Deans brothers and a good welcome at Riccarton just before Christmas in 1844. After a week's rest he headed for Nelson. Tuckett's chart towards the Wairau country led him to rugged and mountainous country. He gave up hope of reaching Nelson by an inland route and during his retreat he fell from the top of a hill to its foot, lay insensible and injured, and recovered to reach the banks of the "Waihau" [Waiau]. He made a raft, traversed some of the Waiau, upset, nearly drowned, and had to exist on wild thistle.

Nearly dead from his privations he reached Motunau. A contemporary report in a Nelson newspaper recorded that at one stage: "He laid himself down exhausted in as open a space as he could pick out, placing his pocket-book and chart in a conspicuous situation, with no hope of ever rising again, and with the very so-and-so satisfaction of thinking that some passer-by might see his body or his bones, and make out whose bones they were from the pocket-book and chart." No doubt sleep restored both hope and energy.

Remember that in November 1849 Eyre and W. J. Hamilton had failed to explore the Nelson-Canterbury route from the north (see page 68). This must have been frustrating for Hamilton because he had climbed Mt Grey eight months earlier and seen the Amuri and other plains. He had reported to Governor Grey that the choice of Canterbury by Captain Joseph Thomas as the site for the Canterbury Association's Colony was a good one. Hamilton had also ventured into the lower reaches of the Waiau and Hurunui valleys, had identified some peaks by Maori names. He had found good grass and soil. J. S. Caverhill, the exploring

runholder (see page 68), made important journeys into the back country of the Waiau from his base at Motunau. Caverhill had been an exploring overlander in Australia. Like Eyre, he was both energetic and restless, experienced, and modest about his achievements.

Captain Thomas had not made his choice lightly. He and his men had crisscrossed the low country of Canterbury between the sea and the foothills, had covered the region bounded one way by the Waipara river and another way by the Ashburton river. He also traversed much of Banks Peninsula. At that stage Thomas was in his forties. He had previously worked with C. Kettle in Otago. One of his men was C. O. Torlesse, an improver on the survey staff. Torlesse made the first ascent of the Rubicon Peak of the Torlesse Range in 1849: a supreme vantage point for a view of the Canterbury Plains.

He was somewhat laconic about his climb: "Very fine. The Big Fellow (a Maori from Port Levy) and I started from Coldstream Pass and ascended the Otarama mountain . . . Arrived at the summit at 4 p.m., not having rested or fed since starting. Warm on East side, bitterly cold on West, there being a strong wind from the snowy mountains. Drank deliciously cold snow water. Sketched plain and hills to the Southward . . . Descended by a shorter route and arrived at John Hay's house at Matariki at 9 p.m." Torlesse was as enthusiastic about the possibilities of Canterbury for settlement as Captain Thomas: "Tuckett must have been blind to pass over this place. As I said to you [E. W. Stafford] — Providence interfered with him and saved this for Canterbury . . . I have been up a snowy mountain and other high hills and have had fine views of the whole place from them besides walking over the greater part of it and measuring 80 miles."

The reference to Tuckett was about his unfavourable report following his brief visit of 1844 to the Waimakariri near its mouth: "The great plain is not worth occupying in small sections."

Fox also supported Thomas. His talent as an artist enabled him to give a graphic view of an exploring expedition, appropriately with the Torlesse Range on the skyline, and closer groups of his party. Torlesse also explored South Canterbury.

With the arrival of Canterbury Association settlers 1851 saw squatters allowed to select land on the plains. Some were more enterprising and headed inland. M. P. Stoddart, an Australian with pastoral experience, went up the Rakaia and with companions visited Lake Coleridge. By 1855 the sheepmen who sought new grazing country had to go behind the foothills, through the river gorges, and examine the

n engraving of 1850 from the *Illustrated London News* of the Canterbury Settlement
om Mount Herbert above Lyttelton Harbour.

n exploring party crossing the Waimakariri River on the Canterbury Plains. The Torlesse
ange is clear on the right. Sir William Fox made this graphic painting.

78

high country beyond. McKenzie, a famous sheep-stealer[1], found a pass from South Canterbury to the Mackenzie Country in 1855, and left legend as well as his name on those tawny acres bounded by a horizon whose mountains rose to Mt Cook itself.

The pioneers in the Rangitata were C. G. Tripp and J. B. A. Acland, whose descendants are well-known farmers in Canterbury today. As Tripp and Acland journeyed beyond the Rangitata Gorge they burned the long snowgrass as they went. Subsequently Acland pushed up the valleys of the Havelock and the Clyde sources of the Rangitata till he had reached great glaciers and marvelled at their moraines and crevassed ice. Both Tripp and Acland were too busy with the demands of their farming to seek further new country, though Acland made other excursions to the glaciers he admired so much.

[1] James McNeish, a modern researcher, is convinced McKenzie was unjustly convicted of that crime.

The heritage of the new settlers included not only new country to be explored but also the knowledge that Maori trails had crossed some of the passes of the Main Divide. The ashes of perished fires; footprints obliterated in places by rock slides and snow avalanches: these contributed to the fascination of the back country. Sit in the evening under the lee of a boulder at a camp fire, hear ruru (the morepork) owl calling across the valley above the rustle of the wind or the rapids of the river, and though the peaks are bleak and lonely it is a solace to know that Maori explorers once passed this way. They too met the challenge of a mountain barrier, and felt the excitement of crossing a pass to unfamiliar gorges below.

Maori legend has it that the first crossing of the Southern Alps was made about 1700 AD by Raureka of the Ngati Wairangi. She was said to have travelled up the head of the Arahura river, home of greenstone, the valued pounamu. At the head of the river she found the pass we now know as Browning's Pass

Above: The Mackenzie Country from Burke's Pass showing the vast expanse of sheep grazing plains.

The Havelock valley of the Rangitata first explored by Tripp and Acland, pioneer pastoralists.

The Arahura valley, home of the greenstone so precious to the Maoris.

She crossed this and descended the mountain valleys. Near the place we now call Geraldine she fell in with a group of Ngai Tahu. When they saw her greenstone — and she admitted there was plenty more in the Arahura across the ranges — a war party gathered. The Ngai Tahu crossed the pass to Westland, fought with Ngati Wairangi, and returned laden with the stone. The significance of this discovery was that it gave a short route from Canterbury to Westland and thus avoided long coastal walks or dangerous canoe journeys.

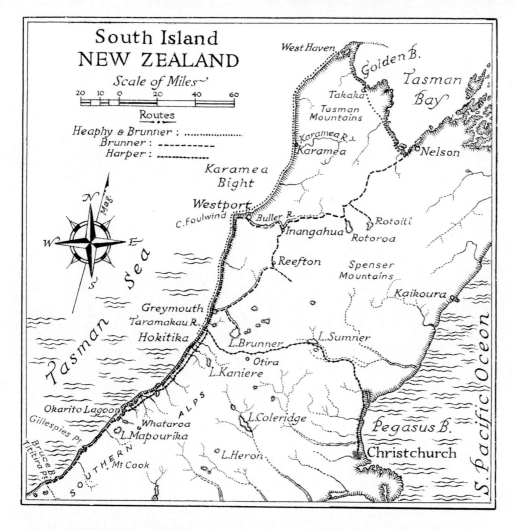

South Island
NEW ZEALAND
Scale of Miles

The first significant Main Divide pass for the Pakeha was one at the head of the Hurunui river in Canterbury leading to the Taramakau in Westland. The Kaiapoi Maoris knew this route. Edward Dobson, provincial engineer, with Mason and Taylor, sheep-run holders, were the first Pakehas on the pass. A newspaper of the period, 1857, noted "A Maori path has been known to exist from the east to the West Coast by gorges of the Hurunui . . . a certain precipitous gully in the gorge has been the obstacle to exploring parties." Dobson and his party crossed to the head of the Taramakau, but the weather was bad and they returned to Canterbury. Two other men visited the pass.

These events prompted young Leonard Harper, a son of the Bishop of Christchurch, to make the first complete transalpine crossing. He left at the end of October 1857 and spent an interesting three months away from Christchurch with a Mr Locke and three Maoris. They left their horses some distance past Lake Sumner after towing their swags in a canoe. They crossed the pass, now mapped as Harper, and met obstacles of scrub and snow. Their descent of the Taramakau valley in Westland was delayed by freshes in the river.

Nowadays this part of the trip would lead to a welcome beer or a hot pie or both at Otira, and perhaps the rest of the journey would be made by rail. But in 1857 Arthur's Pass was not known to the settlers. Further down the Taramakau, and after Harper had made a side trip for a look at Lake Brunner, the river became so tortuous and deep that perforce the explorers made a raft of flax sticks and floated down through a gorge and thus to the Maori pa at the Taramakau mouth. After a visit to the Grey river Maoris, Locke decided to recuperate as his feet were in a bad way.

A local chief, Tarapuhi, travelled with Harper south along the rugged coastline in Brunner's footsteps. They went to a point which may have been at least near Okarito, possibly further south. They lived on eels and birds. Having no tents, they improvised shelters and breakwinds. Now travellers take the main highway to the Haast or fly in a few hours. For Harper and his Maori guide it was a rough-and tumble of crawling round rocks at the base of cliffs pushing over scrub trails past steep headlands, or walking through the soft gravel and sand of the beaches. On the return to Canterbury Tarapuhi walked over the ranges with Harper and Locke. They were ragged and hungry when they reached Lake Sumner.

The importance of this route was underlined by its use by diggers in the goldrushes of the following decade, but it was too indirect ever to be chosen as the way for a stock road or a railway. The Canterbury Provincial Government needed a shorter one. In passing it must be noted that Harper found specimens of gold on the beaches at the mouth of the Grey and the Taramakau rivers. Today the crossing of Harper Pass is regarded as a pleasant tramping excursion, with the only danger the fording of the Taramakau. The track is well marked, and there is a hut for each night of the journey. Perhaps no one

doing that trip can recapture the sense of excitement of Leonard Harper, when he accomplished his adventure. Harper left New Zealand after his law practice failed following a charge of embezzlement. He died an exile in the Channel Islands. His brother George and his son Arthur enter the story of exploration in later episodes.

The only other journey in Westland recorded in 1857 was the coastal one from Cascade Point and Jackson Bay made by shipwrecked whalers who walked right through to Nelson, helped by isolated Maoris with food and directions.

The Harper Pass from the upper Taramakau, first crossed by Leonard Harper and Locke with the Maori chief Tarapuhi in 1857 and subsequently used by gold diggers.

Explorers floating down the Taramakau River, from an engraving in the *Illustrated London News* of 1865.

1857 was a vintage year for some of the interior. John Turnbull Thomson, an experienced surveyor and engineer from Malaya, was then chief surveyor for Otago. He crossed the Lindis Pass, today a key feature of the main highway from Mt Cook to the Southern Lakes. He visited Lake Ohau, and surmised that there was a pass beyond it to the West Coast. He explored the valley beyond Lake Pukaki. This was the first visit to the Tasman valley. He described the majesty of Mt Cook contrasting with the grassy downs down-valley. He gave names to features that were later changed by Haast, who had a genius for taking credit for other people's work. Thomson's work in Otago and Southland will be referred to later in this book, but it may here be emphasised that professionally he was one of the best surveyors who served New Zealand. He was an artist, and a man of considerable humanities.

The 1860s got off to a good start with the arrival of Samuel Butler. He was a curious mixture of bi-sexual man, an "earnest atheist" as one biographer called him, a musical artist, a thinker and a writer. He was the future author of the satire *Erewhon* whose opening chapters describe some of the country and his experiences as explorer.

Butler arrived in Canterbury in 1860. He was in fact a young literary gent from Cambridge whose repressed early life in a Victorian family he recorded with cruel relish in his novel *The Way of All Flesh*. He wished to double his capital as sheepman, and thus secure independence for the future. In this he was successful. His letters published by his father as *A First Year in the Canterbury Settlement* were lively and informative.

Butler had the facility and eye for country of the true explorer. Even from the bridle track above Lyttelton he realised that the ranges described to him as "the Southern Alps" and appearing to him as "rather a long, blue, lofty, even line like the Jura from Geneva" were merely outer ranges and not the real axis. His attitude too was right for an explorer: "As soon as I saw the mountains I longed to get on the other side of them."

His deep enthusiasm for music, dialectic and philosophy made him suspect to his fellow settlers. His aims were both practical, in seeking for new sheep country, and romantic, for curiosity: "The great range itself. What was beyond it? Ah! Who could say? There was no one in the world who had the smallest idea. . . Could I hope to cross it. . . Might I not find gold, or diamonds, or copper, or silver?. . . These thoughts filled my head and I could not banish them." The musing of Butler's hero in *Erewhon* was his own musing.

Samuel Butler at the age of 22 years.

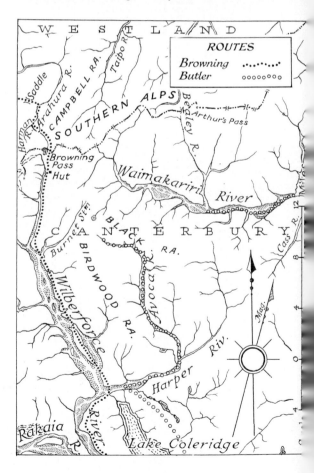

Butler's first trip was beyond Lake Coleridge, where a glaciated range blocked access to a river that he rightly placed, though he did not see it, as the Waimakariri. Later he went up that river, and though he saw a point and pass we now know as Arthur's Pass, he did not cross it because he thought his horse might stray in his absence. "I feel as though I have left a stone unturned", he wrote, "and must, if all is well, at some future time take someone up with me and explore it." It is likely that the place from which he made this entry was near the boundary of the present Arthur's Pass National Park. He also visited the Harper Pass.

Butler's best exploration was based from his hut in the Rangitata, where his sheep-run Mesopotamia took his energies. He could admire a mountain for

The Avoca valley, first explored beyond Lake Coleridge by Butler.

The Waimakariri headwaters as they would have been seen by Samuel Butler on his journey in 1860.

its design as for the pastures on its approaches. He teamed up with John Holland Baker, a young surveyor of twenty years — five years younger than Butler and they tried first from the Havelock branch of the Rangitata for a new Main Divide pass. A typical incident was when both men lost footing in a swift ford. But there was no pass up the Havelock; cliffs and glaciers blocked the way. Future generations of mountaineers had yet to be born who could solve such puzzles.

Some of the cliffs and glaciers that blocked Butler and Baker when they sought a pass from the Havelock branch of the Rangitata.

"... the river narrowed and became boisterous and terrible" was a good description of the Lawrence River given by Butler in his satire *Erewhon*.

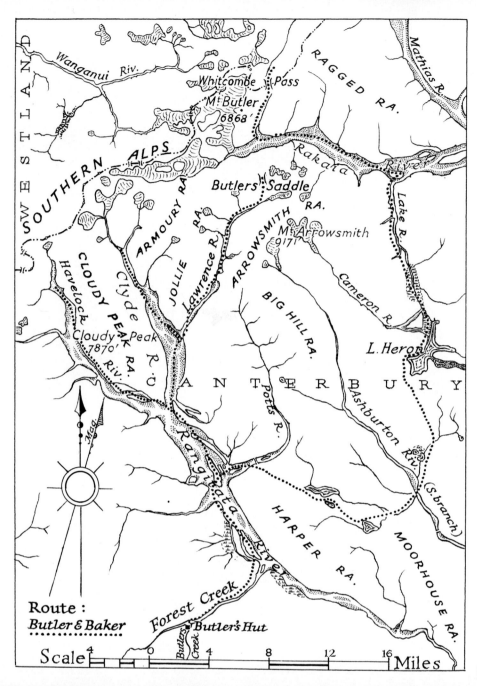

Wanganui Riv.

WESTLAND

SOUTHERN ALPS

RAGGED RA.

Mathias R.

Whitcombe Pass

Mt Butler 6868'

Rakaia River

Butlers Saddle

ARMOURY RA.

JOLLIE RA.

Lawrence R.

ARROWSMITH RA.

Mt Arrowsmith 9171'

Lake R.

Cameron R.

Clyde R.

CLOUDY PEAK RA.

Havelock

Cloudy Peak 7870'

Riv.

BIG HILL RA.

C   A   N   T   E   R   B   U   R   Y

L. Heron

Potts R.

Ashburton Riv.

MOORHOUSE RA.

(S. branch)

Mag.

Rangitata River

HARPER RA.

Forest Creek

Butlers Creek

Butler's Hut

Route:
Butler & Baker
· · · · · · · · · · · ·

Scale

4   0   4   8   12   16

Miles

Below: Butler's Saddle from the Lawrence valley.

Late in January 1861 Butler and Baker tried to find a pass up the Clyde branch of the Rangitata, but once again they found the barrier too high. Another tributary, the Lawrence, was more feasible, but when at last they crawled breathless to the top of a saddle they found they were only on a minor range, and 3,000 feet below was the further obstacle of a glacier river, the Rakaia. Beyond that river lay a Main Divide saddle, and beyond that the blue inscrutable haze of Westland, the terrain of the mythical Erewhon.

The snowy approach to Butler's Saddle from the Lawrence.

...uper Peak and the Whitcombe Pass from Butler's Saddle. Butler wrote in *Erewhon* of this ...ne. "Almost before I could believe my eyes, a cloud had come up from the valley on the ...er side."

The Lake Heron approach to the Rakaia valley.

The Louper Stream approach to the Whitcombe Pass, from the air.

This was the trail to success. Returning to their horses in the Lawrence valley, the two men rode round to Lake Heron, gained the Rakaia, crossed it, and reached the crest of the Divide. They had found a good route to Westland, but did not pursue their advantage, because they saw the way ahead was riven by gorges and cloaked in scrub and jungle. The pass became known as Whitcombe Pass, because a surveyor of that name crossed it to his death by drowning, as will shortly be related. But Butler had proved that a pass did exist, and those of us who have used it have paid homage to his memory as we trudged over its rocky heaps down to the fearful bluffs and torrents. A friend of Butler's wrote to him that he had found a better thing than sheep country — he had found Erewhon, and himself. Butler returned to England with his doubled capital, to his saturnine literary career and his posthumous fame.

Baker did further exploration. With E. Owen in March 1861 he went up the east side of Lake Tekapo in the Mackenzie Country and "found some superior river flats which had not been taken up". Owen wrote "At the earliest opportunity I wrote to my uncle, Archdeacon Mathias, asking him to apply in our names for '15,000 acres lying in the north-east valley at the head of Lake Tekapo'. The claim lapsed as the land was neither sold nor stocked within a year." Owen noted ". . . eventually the country was taken up by a Mr Sibbalds and was afterwards known as Lilybank Station."

From Lake Pukaki the two men rode to Lake Ohau and went some way up both branches of the river that flows into it, but found no grass country worth stocking, so returned down the lake again: "The scenery on these rivers is very beautiful and the hills heavily timbered. From here we had a long ride across country to the Ahuriri branch and rode up the valley in which it is situated until we reached the spot where the birch forest covered both sides of it as far as we could see; then we turned back. We had now explored every branch of the Waitaki without discovering any grass country not occupied, except the small piece we had found at the head of Lake Tekapo.

Lake Tekapo and the Mackenzie Country.

90

The way was set for Haast to continue this pioneer work, though he does not detail the work of his predecessors. With Arthur Dudley Dobson in 1862 he re-explored the Tasman and other valleys. Haast was undoubtedly an energetic character and his travels were more notable for scientific interest than for going "where the foot of man has never trod". Indeed the story goes that when he once voiced such a claim, a shout through the mist was heard from a shepherd: "Hi, mister, have you seen any of my ruddy sheep down there?"

Haast penetrated most of the Canterbury river headwaters and gave an account of them in his book of geology. His work was important to the development of the Canterbury Province, but he was in fact preceded by other men in the glacier country. He comes into prominence later in the story of Otago over the disputed discovery of the Haast Pass. Thus sheepmen had accounted for some of the major journeys. Later, details were added to the maps by surveyors and mountaineers. When next you travel across the Canterbury Plains and see the distant line of the outer ranges, think of the high pasture land that lies behind the gorges and of the men who sought it as grazing for their flocks, and of the dogs that barked defiance at the nor'west wind as it ripped down the valleys and flung the dust from the arid riverbeds.

What of Westland? We have seen that isolated sealers, Brunner, Leonard Harper had genuflected in the coastal scrub as they scratched their sandfly bites. A North Island trader who had passed along in a ship in the 1830s had written: "From the sea, the aspect of the above land is desolate and repulsive in the extreme." The discovery of gold was to change that view and to provide the stimulus for men who would learn to live in the country and to love it for its challenges.

The adventurous expeditions made by men of the calibre of Andy Williamson, who dragged a boat against the current of the Arawhata in 1863, and the complex explorations by the prospector A. J. Barrington and his mates will be described later. For the meantime it is sufficient to know that the discovery of gold in Otago in 1861 was bound to arouse speculation in the possibilities of neighbouring provinces.

Canterbury surveyors were ready to fossick in the Main Divide for passes to Westland. Samuel Butler had reported his Rakaia pass to the survey office. In April 1863 Henry Whitcombe and Jakob Lauper, a Swiss, were sent to cross it. Lauper[1] felt very much at home in the mountains, and his diary recorded: "These mountains and glaciers reminded me of my young days, when often-times, light-hearted and free from care, I had wandered about in just such places."

[1] The explorer Jakob Lauper had features named after him: Louper Peak; Louper Stream. These names were on the maps for so long they became well established. When I discovered that Louper was Lauper it was too late to alter the map names.

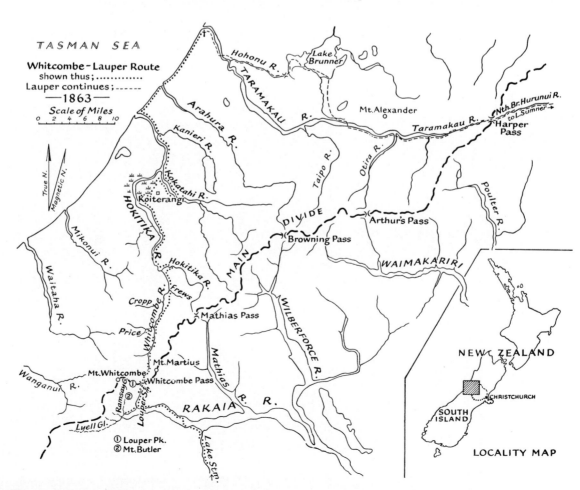

The Ramsay Glacier which reminded Lauper of his young days "light-hearted and free from care." Mt Whitcombe dominates the scene.

The Whitcombe River falls through bush to boulders, hard going for Lauper in 1863.

Their equipment and provisions were not well chosen or adequate; it was evident that Whitcombe had underrated the expedition: they had expected to exist on two biscuits a day, to march six miles a day, and to do without a tent.

Rain and snow made their biscuits a wet doughy mess, and their blankets heavy and useless. Progress was worse than slow. It was small consolation for Lauper to find gold specks in river gravel. After thirteen days of hard going they reached the mouth of the Hokitika river, and a day later found that the pa at the Arahura had been burnt, leaving insufficient food. Weakened by hunger they tried to force a crossing of the flooded Taramakau on a contraption made from old canoes. The surf capsized it; Whitcombe drowned. Lauper survived, and at Lake Brunner friendly Maoris took him to Howitt's survey party. There he rested.

When he ploughed through the snow over Harper Pass, he met some men on the Canterbury side who asked if he had seen anything of two men — Mr Whitcombe and Lauper. " 'You must be mad', I said; 'give me some mutton, if you have any.' 'Oh!' said George (the youngest), 'it is Jacob; now I know him; where is Mr Whitcombe?' 'He is dead,' I answered, and then told them everything."

91

Because James Mackay had in May 1860 bought Westland from the Ngai Tahu for 300 sovereigns and every hint of gold added to the prospects of the region, the search for passes became keener. Lauper's narrative was printed in the *Canterbury Provincial Gazette*. The track across Harper Pass was surveyed, R. P. Bain began his survey of South Westland from the sea, and John Rochfort and Arthur Dudley Dobson did their share of adding to Brunner's map. Dobson made the first sketch of the Franz Josef from the sea.

The Dobson family were indeed important to Canterbury and Westland exploration. In 1864 Arthur Dudley Dobson and his father Edward crossed the Waimakariri-Bealey saddle to the Otira seen by Butler. This Arthur's Pass was the route destined to take the first transalpine road and railway to the West Coast. Albert William Hunt found gold near Lake Brunner that year, and so "the remotest corner of the province" became the El Dorado of hopeful diggers who tramped over the Harper Pass in their hundreds. Dobson had gained information about his

Sir Arthur Dudley Dobson

Dobson's sketch of the Franz Josef Glacier from the sea.

John Gully painted this view of Mts Tasman and Cook from the Tasman Sea in 1875.

pass from Leonard Harper's friend Tarapuhi. Although Cass, the chief surveyor for Canterbury had denied that the Maoris knew anything about the Arthur's Pass to Otira route, it was clear from other evidence that he was wrong.

Gold prospecting in Westland revved up. Miners from the Buller and Nelson added to the throng from Canterbury. The Dobsons increased their activity in 1865. George Dobson, a brother of Arthur's, investigated other passes from the Waimakariri to the Taramakau. Goat Pass from the Mingha branch of the Bealey was proved to be an unsatisfactory alternative to Arthur's Pass. Passes from the Hawdon and Poulter branches of the Waimakariri led to impassable gorges, slips and scrub in the Otehake branch of the Taramakau. Harper Pass was too long and circuitous to be a good route. Parties were sent up to the head of the Waimakariri and the Wilberforce rivers.

The pass used by Raureka in 1700 was explored by Pakehas as the most direct way from Canterbury to Hokitika, now a boom town. John Browning, R. J.

Cattle on the Bealey Flats near the Waimakariri. Contrast this with the lithograph (*above*) from the Canterbury Provincial Council *Journal* of 1865. Both illustrations show Mts O'Malley, Oates and Williams.

A drawing by E. Mervyn Taylor of Carrington Peak at the head of the Waimakariri River.

Browning Pass from the upper Wilberforce valley, with its screes and bluffs as obstacles to progress.

94

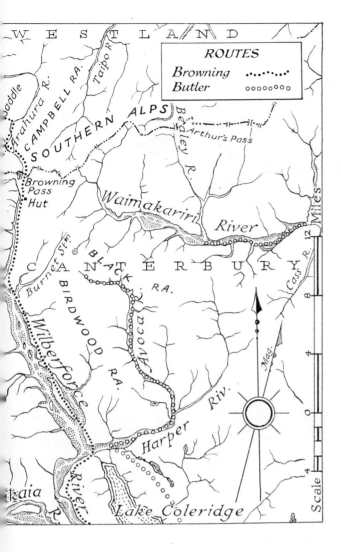

S. Harman and others were recalled from the Waimakariri to survey the Wilberforce and joined forces with Griffiths and Otway. Raureka's pass became known as Browning's Pass. With some backing and filling the pass was crossed to Hokitika. Robert Park, the surveyor from Wellington, was in one party. The steep rock slide from the Wilberforce was a dangerous proposition.

Charles L. Money gave a graphic description of the crossing: "Mr Browning, who was of a daring and impetuous nature, trusted solely to his pick for his safety, while those behind had the advantage of the footholds which we dug with our spades, each one in turn widening the aperture, so that those in the rear could ascend with comparative ease and safety." Money had a voice as well as a thirst for grog, and at the request of Robert Park, named by Money as "Mr Parks, our jolly old commander", he yelled with tremendous vehemence a verse of *The Englishman* which reverberated grandly among the snowy peaks.

Park's paintings give a realism to the cold scenes of scrub and snow in that winter of 1865 at the foot of Browning Pass. His sketch down the Wilberforce to the Unknown corner is a lesson in topographical accuracy, and the spade that dug the steps is clearly shown.

Park's sketch of the Wilberforce valley, with the spade that dug the steps.

Park's painting of the bleak survey camp at the foot of Browning Pass in 1865.

His record of Browning Pass from the Wilberforce compares well with the photograph on page 94.

PLATE 5
Better than any other artist, Petrus van der Velden captured the atmosphere of
stormy sky, spray, gloom, and obstacles in the Otira Gorge. (*Auckland City Art
Gallery.*)

Meins Knob   Mt Goethe   Ramsay Glacier   Mt Kinkel

View towards the sources of the Rakaia from the junction of Whitcombe's Pass Stream

PLATE 6

A fine work by Sir Julius von Haast in 1866 shows what he described as the "view towards the sources of the Rakaia from the junction of the Whitcombe's Pass Stream". The sketch was made above the Louper Stream and shows Mts Prelude, Goethe, Nicholson and Kinkel, with the Ramsay Glacier flowing past Jims Knob to abut Meins Knob. The Ramsay Glacier has since retreated a mile from that point. (*Alexander Turnbull Library.*)

PLATE 6A

Explorers descending the Pelorus River. Charles Heaphy made this painting from a sketch by E. J. Wakefield. (*Alexander Turnbull Library*)

e whata (storehouse) in the bush.

Another routine of pioneer life well described by Mueller was the whata, pronounced "futta", a rat-proof storehouse in the bush: "A place where provisions are kept. . . 1st it must not be exposed to the storms; 2nd it must be watertight and 3rd it must be ratproof. . . The posts you notice must be notched about a foot from their tops and around the thin neck of these posts, strips of tin, from kerosene tins or coffee tins are nailed, so as to prevent the rats from climbing up — the tin is too slippery for them."

Some of the exploits of Douglas belong to the Otago section of this book, but the first ascent of Mt Ionia by Douglas and Mueller in 1885 was the first ascent of a genuine alpine peak in the Southern Alps if we except the Tapuaenuku climb in the Kaikouras by Eyre in 1849. Douglas may have used a miner's pick or a slasher with which to cut steps. Mueller's account referred to two and a half days of hard climbing and the use of the rope on frozen snow. This was more than an alpine ascent, it gave a key

Above and right: The Douglas drawing and the photograph show the Windhover Gorge of the Waitaha valley.

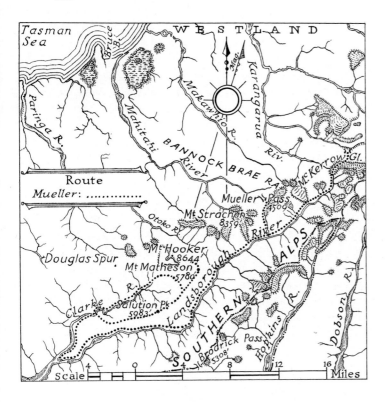

panorama to men who were professional explorers and mapmakers. The following year Douglas made an epic traverse of the Northern Olivine range, a traverse so difficult that the young mountaineers of today find it hard to believe that Douglas could have covered so much country.

Similarly in 1887 Douglas showed Mueller that he was an exceptional climber as when he traversed a razorback on Break-Neck Point in the Landsborough watershed. He was also to gain a good mountaineer as companion; this was Arthur P. Harper, a son of the explorer Leonard of Harper Pass fame.

Douglas must have been a natural as a climber. He could find great joy in his work as when he climbed the low peak of Mt Ragan, a first ascent, from the Waiatoto valley. He did the last two thousand feet without his boots: "The grandest piece of climbing I ever did." His record is such that it could not be equalled today, despite all our advantages of improved equipment, good technique, organised mountain clubs, better access, and air transport. He went up nearly every major river in Westland. His exploration of the Waiatoto found a new Divide pass to the Wilkin. Here again young mountaineers of today have not believed that he found his pass, but I have proved it for my own satisfaction by photographing it from a virgin peak during a recent climb with my wife Dorothy and Stan Conway from the Siberia branch of the Wilkin.

Douglas sketched his pass from the Axius (Te Naihi) branch of the Waiatoto valley to the Wilkin in Otago.

Harper and Douglas at Scott's homestead in the Karangarua in 1895.

Another good piece of Douglas exploration was that of the Copland valley in 1892 when he located the pass later claimed by the English climber Fitz-Gerald and today known as the Copland Pass. Douglas's spirited analogies make good reading in the dry Parliamentary papers in which they were published, sometimes in a corrupted form: "a large rock, hollowed and shaped like an arm-chair, and would just fit the statue of Memnon, only he would have to tuck his legs up"; "I doubt if anything like the Sierra exists out of the moon" were observations made in the Copland valley.

When Arthur P. Harper joined Douglas in 1893 they did some fine work in the Franz Josef, Fox Glacier and Cook river regions. Harper described one camp: ". . . two ragged men on a log in front of a large fire, and a hungry-looking dog lying close by. The men . . . having long unkempt hair and beards, with skins as brown as a penny. In all probability their clothes would be hanging at the side of the fire drying, and they would be sitting with their blankets wrapped round them, smoking their pipes."

107

When Harper and Douglas went up the Karangarua valley in 1894 rheumatism laid Douglas low. Harper continued his trip with Bill the Maori. Later in the 1890s Douglas visited other valleys such as the Whitcombe, spent some time in Hokitika on mapping and report writing. His addiction to drink was a complication in his life. He was awarded the Gill Memorial Prize by the Royal Geographical Society of London in 1897. His last major expedition was up the Wanganui river with William Gunn in 1900. Strokes from 1906 onwards afflicted him and the last years, speechless and paralysed in hospital. were sad ones for a man of such mental and physical vigour. He died in 1916 when the headlines of Verdun were filling the newspapers.

His work was virtually unknown outside Westland till I edited his diaries and letters and wrote his biography *Mr Explorer Douglas*, published in 1957. His endurance and his interest in all features of topographical exploration and the rugged life of the interior make his example one to be followed keenly by men of succeeding generations, and though they cannot attain his record they can but follow humbly in his footsteps and learn from his fortitude that no difficulty is so great that it cannot be overcome. No discomfort can be unendurable if the explorer can keep a sense of humour.

My own mountain career and my efforts as a New Zealand writer were affected considerably by Douglas. In tracing his biography I had to cover some of his

At the Bealey in 1897: G. J. Roberts, Dr L. Cockayne (botanist) and Douglas.

A Douglas companion, Bill the Maori.

routes and to experience some of the dangers met by Douglas. I needed also to photograph some of the scenes he had sketched.

After the death of Douglas, other alpine explorers took up the challenge of untraversed and unmapped valleys. The topographical surveys in Canterbury by T. N. Brodrick and G. H. M. McClure defined the boundaries of sheepruns in the 1880s and 1890s but there were minor inaccuracies to be sorted out. Friends of Douglas such as Dr Teichelmann and guides Jack Clarke and the Graham brothers took their part. The Rakaia-Rangitata region in Canterbury and the tangled ranges between the Whitcombe and the Whataroa rivers in Westland were not only puzzling but were protected, in those pre-aviation days, by bad weather which wrecked some attempts at exploration — for example a probe by Dr Teichelmann and W. A. Kennedy up the Perth river.

By this time mountaineers had to supply the resource to find new passes and glaciers with cols from one valley to another. As the pioneer Sir George Harper told me when he was in his nineties: "You young fellers now climb mountains above passes that we were content to cross. In doing so you find out a lot more about the country for the Survey Office."

There were some interesting chapters written into back-country history. The triangulation of the 1880s when G. J. Roberts linked the Rakaia-Wanganui made it necessary for him to take a theodolite to the top of Main Divide peaks such as Mts Lord and

Malcolm Peak and the Rakaia–Rangitata ranges were climbed by Dr Teichelmann and his guides, and later by young mountaineers of the 1930's.

An aerial view in late summer of the Rakaia Divide from the head of the Wanganui River. The Arrowsmith Range is in the distance.

The sheer cliffs at the head of the Havelock River that blocked Dennistoun's efforts to cross from the Clyde to Westland. This view is from the Garden of Eden Ice Plateau above the Perth Glacier.

Roberts, and he was virtually rubbing his nose against the rocky ramparts of the Arrowsmith Range. A sheep-farmer from Mt Peel in the Rangitata, J. R. Dennistoun was the stimulus for action at the head of the Rangitata. As related before, Samuel Butler had been blocked by cliffs and glaciers at the head of the Havelock and Clyde rivers. Gold prospectors from Westland had made unrecorded journeys from the middle Perth to a Havelock Pass, and a legendary character such as Harry the Whale, of Cook river fame, had joined Alex Gunn and James Bettison in 1875 on such an exploration.

Even G. J. Roberts, doyen of Westland surveyors, thought that a Havelock Pass would lead to the Wanganui and not to the Perth branch of the Whataroa. Dennistoun knew of the Alex Gunn exploration and suspected that his son William Gunn, who had been a Douglas companion in 1900, had also visited the Havelock Pass from the middle Perth in 1905. Dennistoun corresponded with the Gunns. He teamed up with Eric Harper, a Christchurch solicitor well known for his hard running as winger for the 1905 All Blacks.

In 1908 Dennistoun reached a high col on the Havelock Glacier that led to the Clyde valley, but that did not solve any problem of a Main Divide pass. He tried another route. That time he went up the Eric branch of the St. Winifred stream; with Harper he crossed the pass now mapped as Dennistoun. This was very near Gunn Pass, named after the Westland prospectors. The Westland descent was very bluffy, and led to the trap of a gorge in Scone Creek, a Perth tributary. The weather was bad, and Dennistoun decided to retreat back over the Divide to Canterbury. This was a hard trip on meagre rations. Later in the year he returned to his gorge camp site with Peter Graham, where an abandoned puttee was proof that he had actually visited this place in the distress of topographical uncertainty, short of food, and in storms.

Dennistoun holds his abandoned puttee in the Scone Gorge.

110

The generations of the early settlers who had found the mountain passes discomforting had left some record of their feelings. Mrs Nicholas Chevalier, for example, who in 1866 had rode a round trip from the Hurunui, over Harper Pass and back from Hokitika to Arthur's Pass found the latter: "All around bleak weird & dreary, no trees, only lichens & scrub, & patches of snow. Boulders rounded as though worn by water & wind & one could imagine bleak winter snow storms raging & whistling & twisting the telegraph poles which had already marked the progress of man in this wild-ernesses [*sic*]." Her husband, a good artist, tramped up the Waimakariri that year and made the first paintings of its scenic headwaters.

Nicholas Chevalier made these sketches of his wife and party on his 1866 crossing of Harper Pass. On the left, they are descending "The Shoot". Below they are leading one horse over the rough boulders and push another into the river.

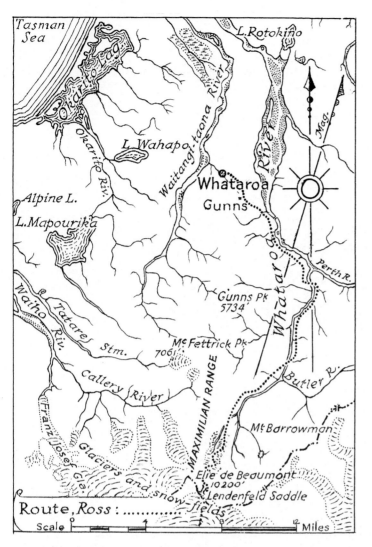

Map of the PERTH - POERUA - ADAMS HEADWATERS, Southern Alps

Succeeding generations had come to accept the back country and the transalpine routes as their own. This was partly due to energetic mountain organisations such as the New Zealand Alpine Club and the Canterbury Mountaineering Club. Young men and women discovered for themselves the attraction of the high country. Now and again they found the bonus of doubtful topography and eagerly noted new passes or proved old ones. The alpine fathers had set them brave examples. In 1897 Malcolm Ross and Tom Fyfe had made the first and only crossing from the head of the Tasman Glacier to the Whataroa and had survived its torrents and its gorges.

My own imagination had been aroused by personal friendship with men like Sir Arthur Dudley Dobson who had discovered Arthur's Pass, and by G. E. Mannering, who had explored the head of the Murchison Glacier. The need for a good map of the Arthur's Pass National Park had from 1929 onwards sent some of us scurrying into odd corners. Four of us camped near Goat Pass at the head of the Mingha branch of the Bealey and though we did not then realise that the pass had been crossed eighty years before, we had the thrill of pioneering and named a new waterfall.

Evan Wilson, a resolute Canterbury mountaineer, made a cold solo climb of Mt Williams in winter, its first ascent, and from the summit saw that the Edwards valley led to a new Main Divide pass to the Otehake. In later years we specialised in the head of the Rakaia and the Rangitata. Four of us made the first transalpine crossing of the Perth Co

John Pascoe's map of the Perth-Adams country is an example of the way in which young mountaineers filled in gaps in survey work.

PLATE 7

The Lindis Pass painted by Nicholas Chevalier on 8 June 1866. The horsemen
face a bleak winter day as snow drapes the tussock spurs so familiar to motorists
today as they drive from Wanaka to Mount Cook. Chevalier was as adventurous
an artist as he was distinguished. Much of his work is in the National Art Gallery.

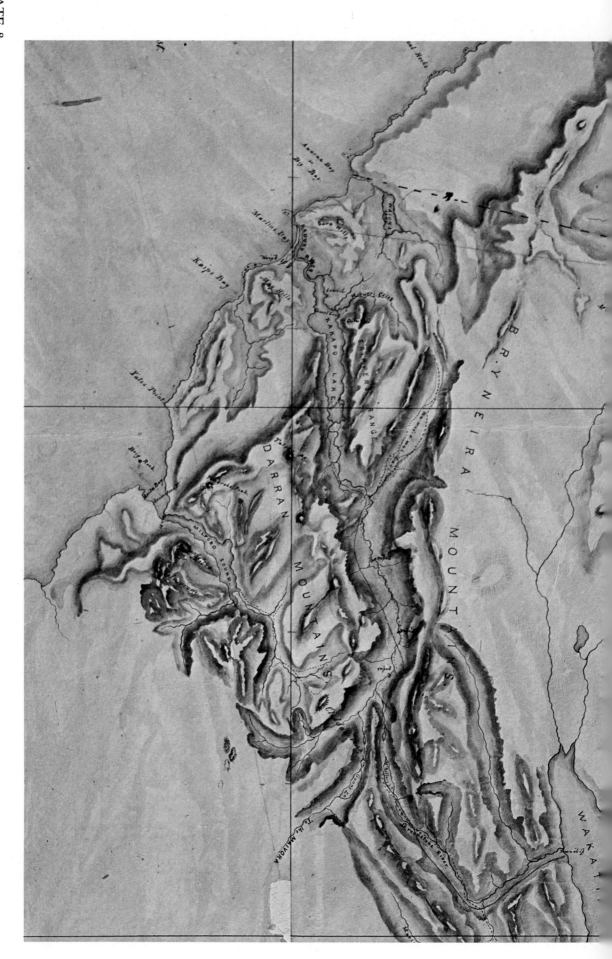

PLATE 8

This fine map of 1863 shows Sir James Hector's exploration route from Martins Bay past Lake McKerrow and up the Hollyford Valley (*see page 133*). It is not known whether Hector did the draughting but he would have supplied the names and positions of some of the features and added to McKerrow's work. This section here reproduced gives "Waiuna Lake" for Wilmot, "Wa-wai-i-wah" for Lake Alabaster, "Kakapo Lake" for Lake McKerrow, and "Kaduka River" for the Hollyford. Hector marked in red the tracks followed as ".....", and a continuous line in red as the best route for a cut trail. Some of the names of 1863 are still in use today: the Darran Mts, Tutoko Pk, Pembroke Pk, Milford Sound, Martins Bay and Mitre (Pk).

Goat Pass, between the Mingha and the Deception valleys in the Arthur's Pass National Park.

Boulder travelling in the flooded Perth valley during its first traverse in 1935 by Canterbury mountaineers.

and thus were the very first men at the head of the Perth. Foul weather denied us much joy, and the rivers gave grave physical danger, but we found in the course of the trip that there was a large glacier plateau that we named the Garden of Eden because it was on the Adams Range. The next season another four of us camped on this plateau, made new climbs, descended to the head of the Adams branch of the Wanganui by an icefall that has since retreated into half its size, and made an adventurous crossing out to the West Coast which involved pool swimming with packs on, sidling above a gorge, going without water for thirty-six hours, and generally getting whiskered and unkempt.

Other corners of this country, namely the head of the Poerua river, were explored by other parties. Gradually we could feel that we knew all the country we had inherited from the pioneers.

113

114

Respect for the Harpers, Whitcombe, Lauper, and Douglas sealed our determination to continue their work and to record it in club journals and other publications. Similarly some parties made marathon crossings such as a series of passes from Arthur's Pass to Mt Cook. Geologists such as James Macintosh Bell and P. G. Morgan did detailed work on geological maps and wrote fascinating reports — all grist to the mill of the young mountaineers in Depression days. Deer killers and hunters too covered parts of the high country of Canterbury and Westland and pooled their knowledge with other mountain men.

The rough terrain and wet weather of Westland tested the stamina of the mountaineers and stalkers as they had tested that of the surveyors and gold prospectors of the pioneer era. Thus the stories of explorers of different generations have a common unity and purpose: to wrestle with the unknown, and, in doing so, to bring courage to it. The rewards are in better knowledge of self, appreciation of companions, the joy of struggle and the determination of values. The maps have recorded the names of many of the pioneers.

Consider the ranges Torlesse, Butler; the passes Browning, Harper, Whitcombe, Arthur's, Harman, Dennistoun, Gunn; the peaks, Baker, Whitcombe, Louper, Douglas, Roberts, Evans. A. P. Harper, Brodrick, McClure, Teichelmann, Mannering; and the glaciers Douglas, Evans: they all remind us of forerunners. A knowledge of the origin of place names is a useful background in a holiday amid unfamiliar scenes. New Zealand has shown that islands can make men and women who are pioneers: it does not always have to be a continent.

The terminal of the Douglas Glacier at the head of the Twain (Douglas) River in South Westland.

Otago and Southland

As elsewhere in New Zealand, there is grandeur and contrast in a relatively small compass in Otago and Southland. The dramatic open spaces of the open central region with their tawny tussocks and grey schist rocks were so different from the steep fiords and forests far beyond the hills. Sealers and surveyors, pastoralists and cattlemen, gold diggers and scientists, hermits and mountaineers all wrote their pages. The economy of trade and goldfields, farms and industry reflected the variety of experiences needed for successful settlers in this lower part of the South Island.

Life in a sealers' camp from Edmund Fanning's *Voyages*. Sealers were too busy on the coast to make journeys of inland exploration.

Captain James Cook's second expedition of 1773 surveyed Dusky Sound. Some members of the expedition went ashore and climbed bushed spurs to gather information or specimens. This staged the opening of European exploration. Twenty years later Captain Raven gained shelter and many skins from his base in Dusky. Further north, Cook had described the mountains as ". . . a prodigous [*sic*] height. . . nothing but barren rocks, cover'd in many places with large patches of snow which perhaps have laid their sense [since] the creation."

A flax trader, Robert Williams of Sydney, roamed inland from the Bluff in 1813. Captain Edwardson of the *Snapper* attempted to go inland from Chalky Inlet in 1822-3. It was small wonder that the French narrator Jules de Blosseville of the *Coquille* wrote from hearsay that the West Coast down there in Fiordland was ". . . one long solitude, with a forbidding sky, frequent tempests, and impenetrable forests". De Blosseville also referred to the long stays of the sealers at stations which enabled them to do "continual exploration". It is unlikely that sealers made any significant journeys because the nature of their work tied them to the coast. In fact, another forty years had to elapse before any substantial inland exploration was accomplished in Fiordland.

The scene must now move to the Otago east coast to the visit in 1843 by Edward Shortland, Protector of Aborigines. His predecessor Johnny Jones, whaler and farmer of Waikouaiti, had plenty of preoccupation without having to traverse coasts or walk inland. Shortland interpreted for Colonel Godfrey, Land Commissioner for the South Island, who had to examine land claims and sales because of the recognition of Maori title under the Treaty of Waitangi. In September Shortland was free to wander from Andersons Bay in Otago Harbour to the Taieri Mouth and Plains, of which he held a poor opinion. His visit to Waikouaiti gave him a chance to travel with Jones to Southland, but his more important journey was to head north towards Banks Peninsula. A blanket bought him the service of a Maori guide. A crossing of the Waitaki river in 1844 on a raft gave

him acquaintance with Huruhuru, who sketched a map of some of the interior lakes of the South Island. This information about the inland lakes and some of the transalpine passes showed how well Maori explorers had covered country. Near Timaru Shortland met Bishop Selwyn, who was on his way south.

Frederick Tuckett, surveyor from Nelson, was chosen to select a site for a proposed New Edinburgh settlement. We know that he rejected Canterbury. In searching for suitable country in Otago and Southland he found that rank vegetation obstructed him. He sailed to Moeraki, keeping as far as possible to the coastline, though he noted that whaling parties had been up some rivers in whaleboats. In Foveaux Strait bad weather kept his vessel from landfall, but on his return he saw enough of the interior of Otago to claim that it was good for the new settlement. The New

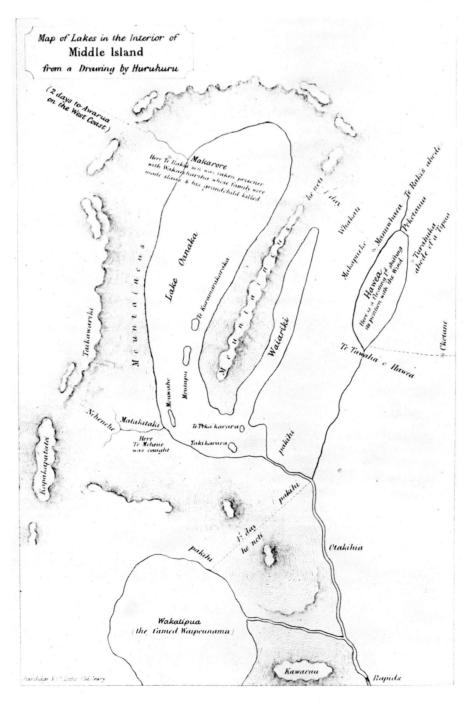

Huruhuru's map of 1844 as published later by Edward Shortland.

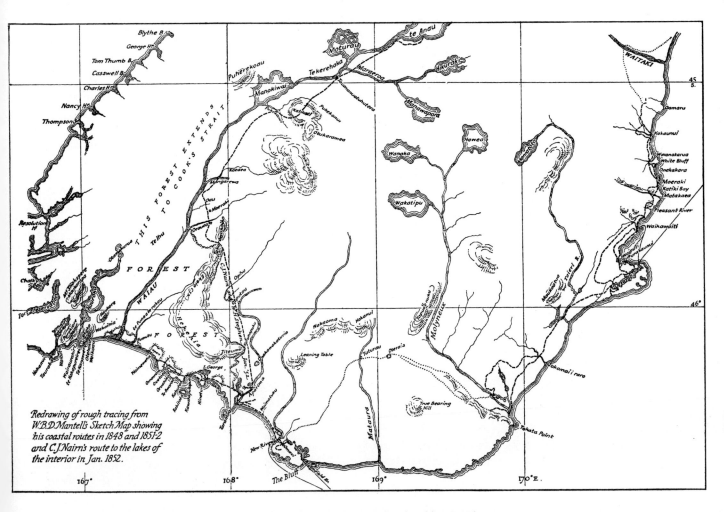

A redrawing of the rough tracing from W. B. D. Mantell's sketch map showing his coastal routes in 1848 and 1851-2. It also shows C. J. Nairn's route to the inland lakes in January 1852.

Zealand Company responded and bought the Otago block from the Maoris in July 1844.

Further exploration had to wait until 1846. Charles Kettle, surveyor, climbed a hill in 1847 from the Taieri Plain where he saw 700,000 acres of grassy downs ideal for grazing sheep and cattle. W. B. D. Mantell arrived in 1848 to settle the boundaries of the Maori reserves, and walked from Kaiapoi to Dunedin. At the Waitaki he went some thirty miles inland as shown by the sketch map. W. J. W. Hamilton, of the *Acheron* survey, who has entered these pages in Canterbury and with Eyre in Marlborough, then made progress in 1849 in Southland, where he found the Oreti country favourable. His journey in the following year from the Bluff to Dunedin, gave him good impressions of the land near Mataura, which grew fine potatoes. In 1851 Kettle made another inland foray. Mantell made an important expedition that year to Southland to report on its potential capacity for settlement and his efforts continued into 1852. He gave a detailed description, in his new capacity as Land Commissioner, of the vegetation and wildlife of the country traversed. His sketches too are valuable

evidence of the period and its Maori occupation.

1852 was also notable in that C. J. Nairn, W. Stephen, and Pharazyn followed Mantell's trail, which they varied by taking a Maori route to Lake Te Anau. They had routine trouble with floods and unstable Maori rafts, delays caused by the guides' pursuit of eels, and the numerous physical obstacles to foot travel. On 27 January Nairn recorded: "Mr Stephen and I went about 5 miles up the Eastern shore [Lake Te Anau] wh. we found very fatiguing; in some places loose sand and small boulders, in others boulders packed close on soft mud which gave under our feet."

Nairn described the other side of the lake: "The Western shore is formed by the snowy alps with grand lofty peaks and pinnacles, domes and cones, rents and clefts on all sizes and forms." They refused to use the Maori raft on the return down the Waiau: "Natives very tired, complaining very much." They later joined Mantell and returned to Dunedin with him. The map on this page shows their route and some of the Maori place names for the lakes.

This positive Maori information must have aroused

117

at least curiosity and possibly lust for grazing land in the minds of those who studied it. Nathaniel Chalmers, later a magistrate in Fiji, was in September 1853 a farmer in the Clutha district. He had "previously arranged, with old Reko, the Maori chief of Tuturau, to take him to look at the country up the Mataura. . . . I asked Reko of what nature the country was as you go north, and he replied, 'Just the same as this in front of us', so we bargained that he should show me the country and that in payment I should give him a 'kohoa' (that is, a three-legged pot)."

Chalmers loaded himself up with the pot, a gun, shot, powder, salt and a blanket. Two days after he had arrived at Tuturau, Reko, Chalmers and a Maori who had run away from the Kaikoura Ranges, left for the interior. The Maoris took spears. The diet would be eels and ducks. As they tramped up the Mataura Chalmers set fire to any long grass which impeded their progress; after five days Chalmers climbed " . . . a very high jagged range alone, and saw a lot of water and snowy mountains a very long way off in the distance about north-west. On my getting back to camp I asked Reko, and he said, 'That water that you saw was the Wakatipu water!' Then I asked, 'How are we going to get across?' He replied that we would go down by a long spur and cross the river that runs out of the lake by a bridge of stone."

This was the natural bridge. Further down river they reached the flats above Cromwell. Chalmers tramped along in sandals made from flax or cabbage-tree leaves. Thus he became the first white man at Wanaka and Hawea. His reminiscences were vivid: "Then toiling along very tired but still getting ducks and eels (it was lucky I had brought salt with me) we reached the Wanaka Lake. We left the lake on our left and, making a small korari raft, crossed the river and went on till we reached Hawea. Here I gave in (for I had been suffering for many months from chronic diarrhoea) and felt too fagged to proceed further. Reko said that two more days' hard walking would bring us to the Waitaki; but I had had enough, so we sat down to think out the shortest way to get back."

They made a raft from flax, and paddles from driftwood. They paddled down the Clutha so rapidly that Chalmers could hardly credit his speed. "When we came to the gorge a little below Cromwell, and below the junction of the Kawarau, my heart was literally in my mouth, but those two old men seemed to care nothing for the current. Eventually we reached where the town of Clyde now stands, and then our troubles were over." They took Chalmers to country that he knew. For fifty-seven years the details of this trip were not published, but other pasture seekers must have known about it from hearsay.

Other runholders pioneered stations and took up grazing land in the interior. A fine booklet by Herries Beattie, *The Pioneers Explore Otago* was printed in 1947 and gave many details of shadowy figures and mysterious events. One odd character was Dr Schmidt, who conned money from the Otago settlement fathers. It was said that the Otago Provincial Council voted him £100 to explore Otago for science, to find a route to the West Coast and to traverse ranges from the Fiords to Canterbury. But he died, presumably from starvation, and his bones were never found.

The Otago Province attracted sheepfarmers to its hinterland and wisely left them to pursue knowledge beyond the ranges.

In 1856 John Chubbin, John and Colin Morrison,

Surveying incidents and personalities sketched by Mantell.

and Malcolm Macfarlane took heart from a map drawn by Reko in sand and went from the Mataura through level country, firing the speargrass and mata-gauri as they went. After three days the party reached the southern end of Lake Wakatipu. Quail perished miserably in the fire. The explorers avoided that fate by taking themselves and their horses into the lake to their necks in the ice-cold water.

An aerial view of Lake Wakatipu showing the relation of its head to the mountain barriers of the Dart.

Lake Hawea, an important point in some of the early exploration journeys.

John Turnbull Thomson made magnificent expeditions in the following year. His experience in the Indian survey was useful in Singapore. His work in Otago and Southland was even more significant. The first trip in the last three months of 1856 was from Dunedin to Southland, where he selected the site for Invercargill and laid out the town and the port.

With Alex Garvie as assistant, Thomson began his survey operations after bad weather and delays in getting more staff. He was fascinated by the bird life. On 16 January 1857 he wrote: "We started with packs on our backs . . . on penetrating into the forest reminiscences of similar scenery traversed on similar duties in the tropical East returned forcibly to the memory." When his dog barked, Thomson noted a tui as the cause: "This feathered individual was seen perched on a tree close by, uttering subdued notes, interluded by harsh and suppressed screams. To this soliloquy the dog was enuciating his violent objections, but our parson bird being beyond reach held on his discourse with much nonchalance. Altogether this bird is a most remarkable one: clothed in feathers of deep black from head to foot, he wears a most grave and sacerdotal aspect. This is not all: he bears out closer the clerical resemblance by the possession of two white feathers under his chin."

The men found the mosquitoes and blowflies most unwelcome. Thomson found it necessary to concentrate in examining the farming country between the Aparima and Mataura rivers. It had been a hard pull in a "leaky and ill-formed" boat up the Oreti river. Eels were on the menu because the beef had become flyblown. When he traversed the Waiopai plains in February he wrote: "As we have gradually lost plates, knives, and forks, we are now existing in the manner of savages, boiling our flesh or fowl in our tea-can (called a *billy*), kneading our dough in waterproof cloaks, and baking our bread in the embers of our camp-fire. Our table is the grass, and our plates a few leaves, our seats a stone or log of wood." Beds were the ground places; meals were damper and tea.

Thomson must have liked this gypsy life: "There is something exhilarating in daily coming on new country, and in descrying new objects of interest. We are now beyond the range of the white man, and the country is utterly desolate of inhabitants, the aborigines having long ago given up their traffic with the interior. The country is now becoming more interesting, as we are in the midst of high and picturesque mountains having level and fertile plains, and valleys at their feet. There is also a great extent of forest to the north, on the slopes of the Eyre Mountains. A valley leads north, low and easy to look at; will this lead into the interior?"

J. T. Thomson, c. 1860

The party camped at the foot of Paiherewao or Mid-Dome, described by Thomson as "Dome Mountain". His narrative proceeded with the zest of the genuine explorer: "To the N.N.E. an opening appeared through which no high land was visible: I conjectured this then to be the pass into the Central districts at present entirely unknown to the European, and but vaguely described by the Moari [sic] . . . the panorama of the Dome mountain is truly grand, presenting to view as it does the snow-clad and serrated outline of the Eyre mountains."

He further wrote: "With our long travel over shingle, our horses are knocked up, and Drummond is in boots without soles, and all our trousers are torn to rags. Lindsay shot a duck, which was a great relish to our sugarless tea."

On 11 March they climbed Centre Hill: "In the valley of the Waiau I saw two pieces of water, distant about 12 miles; these no doubt are the Teanau Lakes; but another is said to exist farther north." His notes referred to Lake Wakatipu as a source of the Mataura, the Jacob and the New rivers. He compared the scenery from the top of the Slate Range as ". . . quite Alpine, imitating in wildness the valleys of Savoy." It must be remembered that in 1857 there were no cultivated fields and green pastures in Southland.

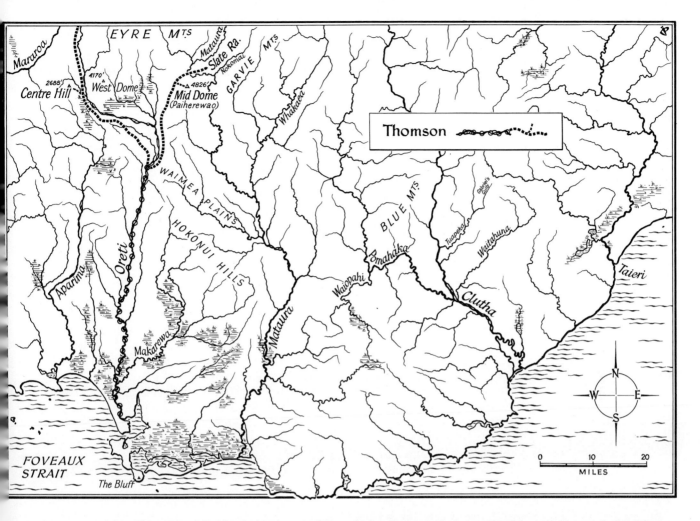

Now and again Thomson harked back to his memories of survey life in Malaya: "The Indian Survey officer is clothed in snow white from 'sola topi' down to canvas pipe-clayed shoes. He smokes his perfumed 'hooka' or the fragrant 'manilla' with an air of listless satisfaction. When he walks on duty he is followed by a 'Piada' carrying an umbrella to shade him from the sun. . . The slightest weight distresses him — he does not even carry a purse. He has hundreds of luxuries at his command; but does he enjoy them?" He gives a dramatic contrast to the New Zealand mapmaker: "The Colonial Surveyor in these regions is clothed in fustian trousers and blue shirt, Panama hat, and stout hob-nailed shoes. He is not known from his chainman . . . he has a hundred things about him . . . and then his 'swag' contains his tent, blankets, and change of clothes. These with his theodolite he carries on his back, and walks away through bogs, 'creeks', and scrubs, at the rate of 3 miles an hour. He cleans his shoes once a month with mutton drippings, and he lives on 'damper', salt junk, and oceans of tea.

"In this land of equality he shares bed and board with his men, but they are not of the common sort, for 'the service' is popular among the enterprising colonists, and he has to pick. They are men that know

their place and duty. Having partaken of the bitters and sweets of both services pretty freely, I must state that upon the whole, as surveyors are made to be killed, I prefer 'dum vivimus' cold air and stout appetite to a hot air and general prostration. I prefer the homely enjoyments of colonial life."

Thomson was back in Dunedin before the winter of 1857 set in. His account in the *Journal of the Royal Geographical Society* was a fine stimulus to new settlers who were skilled farmers. There were times when the pastoral men were neck and neck with survey parties in the same region. Before we consider Thomson's next major trip, from October 1857 to January 1858, pause to look at the exploits of the Shennan brothers, Watson and Alexander. They were from Scotland. Although they admired Dunedin and its port they realised that so little was known about the interior that they could seek land for themselves. They had to wait for horses to arrive from Sydney.

Beyond the Tokomairiro Plain was no-man's-land. The Waitahuna river country was good for sheep but had too much scrub for the brothers. Watson Shennan recorded: "Going on over the ridges there was some nice open country between the branches of the Tuapeka River, and I pitched camp one night

121

in the gully afterwards called Gabriel's Gully, little thinking of the wealth that was buried only a few feet under the ground. Had I suspected the presence of gold, I might have given up searching for sheep country. Later I found the country too rough to get any nearer to the Molyneux River, so kept pretty well up the ridges on the open country. . . "From the top of the Knobbys I had a splendid view of the Manuherikia Valley, presenting a most beautiful landscape — quite a change from the country previously traversed."

He told his brother that this was indeed the promised land. That night they camped on the bank of the Manuherikia river. They crossed the Clutha and traversed upstream from the place we now know as Alexandria to that of Clyde. Later they traversed more ranges and saw the Maniototo plain to be an extensive one. After two weeks' exploration provisions ran low, so the brothers descended to Dismal Swamp, and crossed the Lammerlaw mountain back to Tokomairiro. Watson Shennan said that the granting of grazing rights for the blocks of Galloway and Moutere had fulfilled the purpose of their exploration.

Now, back to J. T. Thomson. He left Dunedin on 14 October with two packhorses, tent, equipment and a month's provisions for three men. In November he crossed the Horse Range to the Shag river and found a good route to the Manuherikia. He recognised the Eyre valley and the Slate Range from his earlier explorations, avoided the flooded Taieri by turning to the east, and returned to Dunedin at the end of the month.

Once again the Maori Reko's information was the key to Thomson's success. He journeyed up the Waitaki river to the grassy flats of Omarama and took a tributary of the Ahuriri to lead him to the saddle we now know as the Lindis Pass. He climbed a nearby mountain, saw a host of alpine peaks, admired the new pasture country below, and endured 85 degrees, characteristic of those parts in summer.

After crossing the Lindis Pass Thomson's party went with him up Black Knob Mountain that he later renamed Grandview, 4,797 feet. He was spellbound by the Hawea lake, some of the shores of more distant Lake Wanaka, the branches of the Clutha sustained by that lake, and, most important of all, he named Mt Aspiring, an act of imagination as well as perception. Later in December they rode to Lake Ohau, thence to Lake Pukaki and up its western shores. His paintings of the period show the excitements of crossing flooded rivers, the spectacle from Mt Grandview, and the prospect from a spur looking up the Tasman valley.

Thomson gave a lively description of Mt Cook, he named Mt Stokes, and must have been disappointed when Dr Haast later changed Stokes to Sefton. Thomson returned to Dunedin in January 1858 after further observations. He had covered nearly 5,000 square miles of pastoral country. His newspaper accounts aroused further interest from sheepmen and it was not long before the country was stocked.

There was still a corner of Otago Central to be explored: between the Slate Range and the Rock and Pillar Range. Alexander Garvie went on a reconnaissance survey of the missing piece of the puzzle.

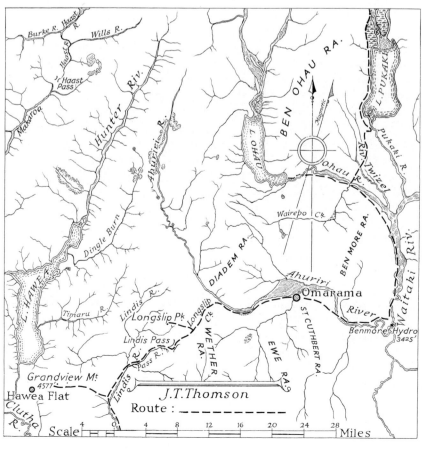

123

In February 1858 his party traversed from the West Taieri to the present site of Alexandra at the Manu-herikia-Clutha confluence; in the following month he led from the Waipori to the Tuapeka and linked with Thomson's Southland triangulation. James Buchanan, in this party, found specks of scale gold. Thomson reported the discoveries but the Provincial Council did not stir.

Certainly the Provincial Council had offered a reward for a payable goldfield, but the most influential newspaper would rather have the quiet life than the roar of the Victorian goldfields. For some two years the efforts at exploration would not be aimed at gold discovery but as a routine for squatter men and surveyors. There was just about a photo finish in the progress of Wakatipu exploration.

Thomson crossing the Ohau River in 1857. He painted this scene twenty years later.

Thomson's painting of Mts Cook and Tasman from a rocky spur above the Tasman valley past Lake Pukaki.

Donald Hay, an Australian, had the qualities characteristic of the enterprising sheepman of this period, and there was a good Gael under the Australian tan. He travelled in 1859 to the Nokomai with D. A. Cameron but when he was ready for solo work he bought a pony and equipment, gun, ammunition, provisions, an axe, a pot and calico oilcloth. Like many of his kind he could write well about his experiences: "It was reported that a gentleman from the North Island had constructed a moki (raft) but the prevailing winds were so strong that he had to abandon the attempt to navigate the lake . . . I searched the south end of the lake, and to my joy and surprise found the moki hidden in the bushes. I improved on it by adding korari sides and round bundles of the same material to strengthen it and form a seat in the centre. I then cut out two oars or paddles, and made rowlocks with two forked sticks, and drove them through the sides of the moki."

Hay paddled along under the shadow of the mountains on the west side, enjoyed eating a weka, camped and later crossed to the east side. The next night he lit driftwood fires on either side of him to keep himself warm. He recrossed the lake after another stormy night and sailed along the south west side. He was forced to land at Beach Bay, Walter Peak, where he dragged the raft on shore to let it dry out to recover some buoyancy. After a day's rest he climbed high to the level of the spring snow to get a view, and varied this by an attempt to traverse the shores of the lake till he was blocked from fording the Von river by the swiftness of its torrent. He was the first Pakeha to discover that the lake had a north arm.

He paddled back to the site of Queenstown, tramped past a new lake, later named for Bully Hayes and not alas Donald Hay. West of Hayes Lake he was blocked by a narrow gorge and sheltered from a snowstorm in a cave. This truly intrepid man crossed the lake once again on his moki using moonlight as his guide. He warmed his numbed limbs by lighting a fire of dry leaves. In the morning he roasted a kaka in the ashes. He had little flour left and no salt.

Hay summarised his adventures: "I was on the lake and in its vicinity about 14 days during my last trip. I had no fear while cruising in my frail bark, but I had to exercise caution, as my craft became saturated with water so that I was in it ankle deep and had to haul it up on the beach to let it dry. Occasionally my legs and feet swelled a little, and the dazzling snow and glittering water made me partly snowblind; otherwise I was all right. When I attempted to ford the flooded river I was afraid to take my 'boat' in case I should lose it in the rapids, and there was no materials in that part to make another; and I tied my gun and all I possessed as high on my shoulder as I could and attempted to ford the river, but on making the attempt I found I was being carried away by the stream, and was in danger of getting my ammunition wet and thereby lose my life for the want of food and fire to keep me alive at night. I hadn't the slightest fear, and all my anxiety was for food and fire."

Hay explained why he left New Zealand: "On arriving at Dunedin I went to the Land Office and gave a sketch of the country I wanted, which had been applied for by someone in the office, with the view of selling it. After getting the lines of the tracing altered in the office, I made an offer to the party whose name appeared on the map, which was refused. I then embarked for Victoria." He commented finally: "I cannot be expected to give the names of the various rivers at that early date, but my isolation on the lake and its vicinity is almost photographed on my mind."

While Hay was making his epic cruise on the lake, D. Cameron's sheep were slowly perambulating their way from the Bluff to Wakatipu right up against the south of the lake, while the shepherds scoured the Kawarau face. Hay must have been very disappointed that his hard journey came to nought so far as he was concerned. (Think of that, you holidaymakers in Queenstown, when next you take a launch up the lake on a glorious day to the head: as you lean over the side and gaze at the ripples on the lake, consider a pioneer on a flax raft in winter with the snowy ranges outcropped with rock looking so coldly down on his efforts.)

The surveyors too were active in this country in 1859. They worked hard west of Wanaka. In particular Edward Jollie and W. S. Young made expedition between 1857 and 1859. The Otago-Canterbury boundary was in dispute; more needed to be known about the Clutha headwaters. Young wrote reminiscently in a letter: "We travelled up the Waitaki and down the Lindis to the Hawea Lake. On the second occasion Mr Jollie procured as a guide from the Waitaki kaik [village] a very old but strong and intelligent native named Kawana, who was familiar with the inland country and the river system. On the second journey we managed to ford the Hawea River and reach the Wanaka, and at night Kawana told us he used to live at a large lake to the southward called Wakatapu . . . On the third occasion we reached the western shores of Lake Wanaka, but did not take the old Maori back with us this time. We explored to the head of the Matukituki River

The Matukituki valley behind Lake Wanaka was traversed by good surveyors and fine explorers; among them, Jollie and Young, McKerrow and Goldie, Hector.

and also penetrated a deep valley a long distance in a southerly direction." This valley to the south was the Motatapu; it overlooked part of the Shot-over. Jollie acted out his name: from the top of the mountain of the Motatapu he said, "Thomson has called the mountain Aspiring; we must call ours 'Perspiring.'" Jollie was the surveyor who in 1852 had pioneered in Marlborough. Young later became a key man in Haast's party on the Haast Pass.

Lake Wakatipu was a long lake. The claims to famous firsts in respect of its exploration must include that of David McKellar who was said to have gone up the Oreti alone, followed down the Von, climbed a spur and seen the upper part of the lake in 1858 which takes him before Hay. McKellar was active elsewhere in 1861. But the events of 1860 must now take precedence.

G. M. Hassing got a contract to supply sawn beech timber for a sheeprun in the Wanaka region. With H. S. Thomson, a local man, he went up the Maka-rora source of the lake, and burnt the mass of cabbage trees, flax and fern which was growing to a height of eight to ten feet above decayed vegetation.

The most important event was the opening up of the large mountainous pasture block between Wanaka and Wakatipu. This began when in January 1860 six men and a cook, fifteen horses and a mule, left

Oamaru. They trekked to Wanaka and decided to head up the Cardrona valley. Only W. G. Rees and N. von Tunzelmann stayed the course, which was a tough one.[1] When they reached the top of the Crown Range, after two attempts, they saw the lake (Wakatipu) gleaming far below: "They pushed on down the hillside, which was now very steep and dangerous, and slid down the last slope on their hands and knees, whilst their horses scrambled down as best they could. The country was covered with matagowrie and speargrass, and consequently their limbs were scarred and bleeding. They camped a night where Arrowtown now stands, and next day had great difficulty in forcing a way through the prickly vegetation to Lake Hayes. At the Shotover they encountered a quicksand, but got through and pushed on up the side of the Kawaru to the so-called falls. . . . They climbed Ben Lomond or an adjacent height, but could not see the head of the lake, but they did discover the tarn known as Moke Lake."

At the lake they made a Maori raft of driftwood, and pushed it round the shores. After a climb up scrub and spurs they saw the very head of Wakatipu, and saw it more clearly than had Hay or McKellar from the opposite side of the lake.

[1] *The Pioneers Explore Otago* by Herries Beattie (Dunedin, 1947) has these and other accounts here quoted.

125

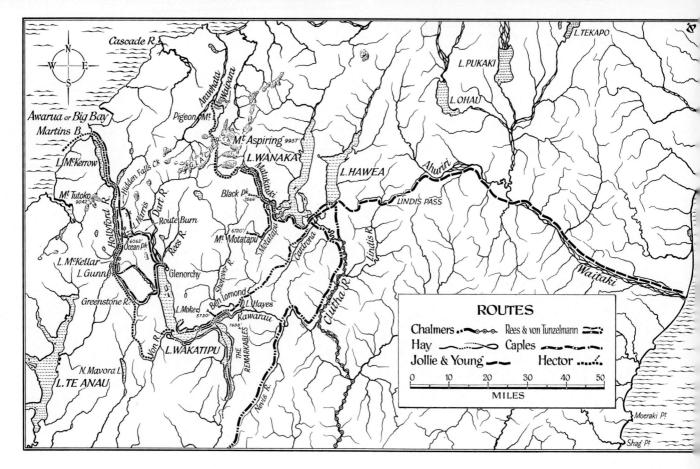

As the career of these men was so rewarding for back-country pastoralists, their names are rightly commemorated in the Von river and Rees valley. But to continue with their adventures! they set fire to the scrub and returned to Queenstown on the raft, chased by the fire. Even when they had caught their hobbled horses and reached the Shotover, the fire was too close for comfort. They returned to Wilkin's station at Lake Wanaka, weary and hungry.

The *Otago Witness* gave an account by Rees in which his estimate of the length of the lake as being sixty-five miles agreed with that given by Hay. He noted of rafting that ". . . nothing but the delightfully warm weather prevented our suffering in health from being constantly wet from the hip downwards." The editorial commended Rees: "It is not every man who could care to navigate an unknown water for six days by means of a moggie [moki] . . . Such was the method of navigation by the first white man who has visited the Wakatip Lake — a fact which it will not be uninteresting to look back upon when the same water is navigated by steamers, by no means an unlikely event in this page of progress."

Rees, of course, would not have denied Hay the credit for his exploration. Rees took up land on the east side of the lake, and von Tunzelmann to the west. Both men prospered in their way. Today Lake Wakatipu has the spectacle of jetboats and aircraft, tourists and ski-tows, proposed luxury settlements, and it seems a far cry back to the frail craft that

was pushed at the rate of three-quarters of a mile an hour by men who were up to their hips in water. Today also there is a good road up the east side of the lake, and parties heading for mountain trips up the Rees valley have good transport.

David McKellar was to graduate to good bushcraft after his initiation to Wakatipu tussocks in 1858. With G. Gunn he made a five weeks' expedition in March 1861. An Invercargill newspaper of the period credited them with the "First Tour of the West Coast" in spite of "unscaleable and precipitous mountains" and "dense birch forests and useless (pastorally speaking)". They saw kiwis, flying parrots (probably keas), and kakas; the only animal life observed was "that concomitant of all Europeans, the RAT".

Apparently the trip started later than they wished because of the delays of shearing. McKellar brought back specimens of what he judged was copper ore. The route from his station at Longridge lay up the Mararoa river, through a gorge, and, hampered by new snowfall, across the Livingstone Range, along it to Lake McKellar and Lake Howden. They saw the Tasman Sea from some mountains climbed: not Blights Sound, as they thought, but leading to Martins Bay. Their return took in Lakes Gunn, Fergus and Lochie, the Greenstone feeder of Wakatipu, and a return to the Mavora Lake. McKellar typified the capable and adventurous runholder and can be compared with his contemporaries such as

Rees. His trip was a good beginning to knowledge of the intricate topography between Lakes Wakatipu and Te Anau.

J. H. Baker and E. Owen, whom we left riding from Lake Tekapo to the Ahuriri (see page 89) were at the same time as McKellar's expedition exploring the Makarora approach to the Haast Pass from Lake Wanaka. Following Hassing's trail, they went beyond it to the crest of the Haast Pass itself, and thus made its first ascent but not its crossing. They were sheepmen looking for sheep country.

Because they did not see open grazing country they were content to write off their exploration as fruitless. And, as a matter for history, the Haast Pass had been crossed in 1836 by a strong party of Maori warriors led by Te Puoho, a contemporary of Te Rauparaha. Te Puoho travelled from Nelson, down the West Coast and up the Haast valley. His objective

was to conquer Otago by this brilliant outflanking move across the Main Divide. Once across the pass, now mapped as Haast, he gained the open spaces of Otago but he left behind him the plentiful birds and eels. When the war party had crossed the Crown Range and made their way down to Southland they at last found good food at Tuturau, near Mataura, in December 1836. The following month they were surprised by a sudden attack led by Tuhawaiki (Bloody Jack) from Ruapuke. This the last Maori battle in the South Island, ended with disaster for the marathon warrior Te Puoho. Only one man in his party escaped to return to Golden Bay.

Skip the years and return to 1861, most famous of all for Gabriel's Gully, the gold discovery that sparked off much exploration. A Nelson paper noted that "a Mr Gabriel Read" had collected seven ounces of gold in ten hours with pan and butcher's knife

Gabriel's Gully in 1862. This lithograph from Vincent Pyke's book about the goldfields shows the conglomeration of tents and devastation characteristic of them.

in the Tuapeka district of Otago. There was an immediate rush to country that hitherto had been the preserve of sheep and cattle farmers. Thus the exploring surveyors would be abetted by gangs of hardy men seeking gold, undeterred by rivers, lakes, mountains, weather, or lack of food. In turn the work of geologists would become of great significance. But the miners would often hold the stage. While they did not make maps, they made journeys of unparallelled difficulty, and even winter would not dam them down.

Naturally friction would arise between the gol miners and the runholders, whose land use would k as threatened by the diggers as much as their reserve of food would be in peril from starving prospector A cartoon of the period shows squatters with stocl whips belting cattle gleefully driving gold digge laden with swags and shovels.

Above: James Brown's cartoon of the squatters driving cattle and diggers.

An *Illustrated London News* version of 1862 of diggers with their swags, picks and other equipment.

The Dunstan diggings, sketched by Frank Nairn in 1863 above the Manuherikia confluence with the Clutha River. The prospectors in the foreground add life to the sketch.

The diggers included some of the most remarkable xplorers who ever stubbed their boots on boulders a the Southern Alps. Engravings of the early 1860s 10w them as bearded and resolute men with huge olls of blankets prominent. Not many were as for- inate as Gabriel Read when he saw gold "shining ke the Stars in Orion in a frosty night", but when ie gold escort returned to Dunedin with 500 ounces f gold, the excitement was intense. It mounted fur- ier when the Dunstan field in 1862 turned out to be nother El Dorado. Canvas townships grew, as itness contemporary illustrations of the future lexandra on the banks of the Clutha. But the roving rospectors were the task force of tough exploration. ew of their deeds were recorded. They came for old, endured for the sake of discovery, whether of nd or gold, and most passed into oblivion. For ery expedition here described there were others out which nothing is known.

The period 1862-64 was particularly eventful in Otago. The Shotover was one focal point. By 1863 Queenstown had grown from a camp on a sheeprun to a noisy boozy prosperous town from which 191,825 ounces of gold had been sent away in the gold escort in its first seven months. Cross-country journeys and companionship were to be the features of many of the epic trips. Nor were the surveyors idle.

In December 1861, James McKerrow, another fine surveyor of the J. T. Thomson stamp, began a series of expeditions that culminated in the survey of over 500 square miles of the mountainous interior of Otago and Southland. John Goldie, in McKerrow's party, left a journal which has filled out some details missing from the official reports. The work was urgent because runs needed map boundaries and not merely those allocated by the occupants: "One gentleman went in search of a run for himself and finds a suitable place, fixes his marks from a certain mountain or stream giving the names to these points or streams himself, then goes and applies to the Crown Lands Board for a run and gets it by paying his licence. In the course of time another goes and does the same . . . perhaps one of his points is from the centre or part of the first applicant's run, thus they have become all locked and intermixed with each other."

The map of the runs would cover up to four million acres and six very large lakes. Sometimes bad weather and fog held them up; other times the descent from a range, such as the Dunstan, was steep and stony for horses. McKerrow's first observation point was from Lindis Peak. By New Year's Day 1862 their horses had swum across the Clutha which the survey party crossed in a kind of box. They crossed the Crown Range, finding it easier than the Dunstan, and descended to the homestead of W. G. Rees. On 6 January they had rowed fifteen miles up Lake Wakatipu and met "Mr von Tunzelmann, a fine looking Russian". McKerrow climbed a high observation point. From the Von river they went over the Oreti, the Mararora and Lake Te Anau. Here McKerrow took more bearings. By the end of the month they had retraced their route to Lake Wakatipu and so back to Lindis Peak, and later the Taieri.

The second expedition was from February 1862. McKerrow, Goldie, another man and "two horses swayed with provisions, instruments and clothes and one was reserved for riding upon". Once again McKerrow climbed Lindis Peak and directed his observations to the country around Lakes Wanaka and Hawea. In March they reached the west side of Wanaka to add to the map prepared by Jollie and Young three years before. Goldie was very impressed by the Matukituki valley, both for its river and for its mountains. He described a difficult and dangerous climb of the Giant's Staircase: "For the first two hundred yards or so we had to creep on our hands and knees, if not serpent-like on our bellies, from the bank of the river till we gained the foot of the mountain, through among thick growing, high over-topping scrub; then we had to scramble up a pile of steep rugged rocks, clinging . . . halting now and again in an eerie swither (perplexity) whether to proceed or return." Another mountain they climbed was 8,000 feet above a snowfield and the view was "truly wild, mountainous and cold looking in the extreme".

On 31 March they camped at the forks of the Matukituki. Goldie described Mount Aspiring as "a peg to mark the boundary line between the provinces of Otago and Canterbury".[1] He wrote that on it ". . . there is a tremendous breadth of frozen snow, which hides his rugged sides from view and

[1] It is wholly in Westland

makes it quite impossible for anyone to ascend it." He noted "We were further up the river and further inland in this direction than ever man was known to be. The country in this district is no use to man unless as a good reservoir to the lowland." They heard many avalanches. In April and May they visited Wanaka and Hawea but missed using Maori information about how to cross the Haast Pass because time was against them. They returned to Dunedin in the middle of winter. The third exploration belongs to the following year.

It is now time to consider the gold prospectors and geologists. In August 1862 Charles Cameron and two fit young men left Dunedin. By October they had reached the north branch of the Routeburn tributary of the Dart. Cameron wrote a letter to a newspaper with a heightened account of the alpine dangers, claimed he had found a new route to the West Coast and asked for a reward. Cameron did further exploration at the head of the Shotover. He returns to these pages shortly as the first Pakeha over the Haast Pass.

Others were interested in the prospect of passes Dr James Hector climbed Black Peak, so prominent from Wanaka, but although he was high above the Matukituki he could not see the sea. In the event he saw a high col at the head of the Matukituki that stimulated exploration a few months later.

1863 was indeed a historic year for Otago exploration. It was also a year of great hardship for all who lived or travelled in the Otago back country because it gave one of the worst winters ever recorded in New Zealand, and people died in blizzards unless they could improvise adequate shelter.

McKerrow's third expedition took place in this year, and was based on Southland. He surveyed Lake Monowai, saw Lake Hauroko in the distance, surveyed Lakes Manapouri and Te Anau, saw Caswell Sound from Mount Pisgah, and returned to Wakatipu Waikaia and Dunedin.

The number, complexity, and importance of the 1863 expeditions in Otago just about needs an order of battle to explain them. Remember also that in Canterbury and Westland, Whitcombe, Lauper and the Dobsons were making their brave endeavours. J Q. Caples is a name to add to such a list. He covered much of the interior, and roved further afield than Cameron. Cutting steps in the ice with a miner shovel, prophetic of other pioneers in those days before ice-axes were used, he made the magnificent crossing from the Routeburn, over the Harris Saddle and the river he named the Hollyford. He made round trip by descending the Hollyford, travelling up the Hidden Falls branch, and crossing North Col, and so back to the Routeburn, and in Cameron's track

The Hollyford valley, well known to surveyors and gold prospectors, and other explorers.

Eager for more knowledge he returned with more provisions to the Harris Saddle and, probably from what is now Ocean Peak, he saw a large lake and smoke to the bush near its outlet. He did not go right out to the coast but tramped back up the Hollyford, crossed the Greenstone Saddle and saw the lakes of Howden and McKellar which McKellar and Gunn had discovered. (Notice how the stories of these explorers cross as inextricably as deer trails.) He made an alpine crossing of the Ailsa mountains to the river now named as Caples, and down to Lake Wakatipu, and up it to the Dart. A chance meeting with McKerrow gave Caples tracings of a map, and encouragement. Caples was still fit and active. He returned up the Greenstone and down the Hollyford to Lake McKerrow and Martins Bay. Hungry enough to eat rats with relish he traversed mountain ridges to Southland. His three months had been exceptionally strenuous for a man alone.

Charles Cameron also made more history as a strenuous man alone.

Charles Cameron in fact was the first European to cross the Haast Pass, and it is likely that he reached the Landsborough confluence. His feat was contested with some bitterness by the biographer of Sir Julius von Haast, who carried filial bias to extremes. Haast and Young and party followed Cameron a few days later in January 1863 in bad weather and under stress from floods. Haast's expedition was accompanied by hardship and was important scientifically because it

ir Julius von Haast.

Right: Douglas made this drawing of the Haast Pass from the Makarora side. It is likely that Charles Cameron made the first crossing of this pass as far as the Landsborough.

actually reached the West Coast, but he should not have denied credit to Cameron, who travelled alone and as fast as a modern deer killer, with the simple gear of the digger and without packers or track-cutters. (This story is given in perspective and in the context of the new Highway Six in my book *The Haast is in South Westland*.) Charles Douglas, like other New Zealanders of the time, was somewhat indignant about Haast's shoddy treatment of Cameron and wrote: "Make some acknowledgement that you do get information from the inhabitants who live about the country." The bronze plaque marking the Haast Pass was set up by the Historic Places Trust to give due credit to the Maoris, to Cameron and to Haast.

Other events of 1863 were the Arawhata trip of Andy Williamson when in June he dragged a ship's boat up the current seeking gold, and the exploits of Captain Alabaster when he rediscovered Lake McKerrow, went up the Hollyford, climbed a peak near Lake Howden and saw Lake Wakatipu. Later Alabaster explored the Pyke and found the lake named after him.

Dr James Hector, a geologist for the Otago Provincial Government was also active in 1863. The first of his major expeditions was momentous for its near-achievement of a first crossing from the Matukituki to the West Coast and for the first use of alpine equipment of rope and ice-axe to overcome the obstacle of a crevassed glacier. Hector had had Canadian experience in 1857 when he discovered the Kicking Horse Pass, later used in the transalpine route of the Canadian Pacific Railway.

Hector took with him L. Rayer, and Sullivan, a reporter from the *Otago Daily Times*. He used his mountain and river experience to great advantage to cross the high col he had previously seen from Black Peak near Wanaka. The party was able to use packhorses as far as Shovel Flat, past the present

site of the New Zealand Alpine Club headquarters hut in the upper Matukituki. Before they had reached the last of the scrub at the head of the river Hector made caches of provisions. An avalanche of snow made its tongue across the river below the Breakaway, scene of a mountain fatality late in 1970. When they had arrived at the Divide pass now named Hector Col, Sullivan's description was: "The high mountains to our right, with their clear blue pinnacles of ice pointing to the sky, and shrouded in enormous glaciers, presented a truly alpine scene, while the whole valley at our feet was completely filled by a glacier occupying an area of about 5 square miles." A "perilous and laborious descent" took them to about 800 feet above the valley glacier.

Hector named the river and glacier the Haast, but later these names were changed to Waipara and Bonar respectively. This area has been subject to a very spectacular glacier retreat, to the point that alpine parties must now avoid Hector's descent, and the valley glacier has left a lake, with icebergs, that will soon dry up and leave a shelf of silt.

On 18 February Hector led his party across the glacier with some acrobatic ice climbing and step cutting. They made a third cache of food. Then the travel was the routine one of bush, gorges, a river grown unfordable because of the volume of new tributaries. Hector was beaten by the final gorge of the Waipara and made a climb over Pigeon Mountain (now Mt Snowden) which took four thousand feet of hard work. They later descended to the Waipara-Arawhata confluence where Nolans Hut now stands. They estimated their distance from the Tasman Sea as eight miles, but it would have been nearer twenty.

The return journey, begun on 24 February, was desperate. When the food was gone and the rivers flooded they had a tough job to ford the river. They crossed back to the Matukituki early in March. They felt the effects of cold, hunger and wetness.

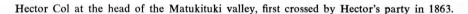

Hector Col at the head of the Matukituki valley, first crossed by Hector's party in 1863.

The subsequent history of the Waipara valley has some highlights including one in which I took part. In 1885 Mueller and Douglas visited the head of the valley, mapped it and gave splendid names: Stargazer, Moonraker, and others. The second crossing of the Matukituki to the Waipara and over the Main Divide had to be made further west because the glacier retreat had made Hector Col so dangerous. This was in 1940 when J. H. Christie, an engineer, and Allan Shannon went down the Waipara and over "Pigeon Mountain" to avoid the lower gorge. Other alpine parties climbed from the head of the Waipara. In 1960 Stan Conway and I repeated the Hector trip with the Christie variation, but with this difference: Conway was mortally ill halfway down the Waipara and we had to press through the lower gorge regardless of its reputation for inaccessibility. We found a good way, and Conway later recovered from his illness. Thus our experiences had linked us with our exploring forefathers.

Hector was still exploration-bound in the winter of 1863. He went up the Greenstone with von Tunzelmann and realised its affinity with the Hollyford. He neither met Caples nor read the newspaper reports of his pioneer work in the Hollyford. He went to Fiordland in the *Matilda Hayes*, landed at Milford to be repelled by the wall of mountains above the Cleddau, noticed Maori fires opposite Martins Bay, went ashore, met Tutoko and his family, and travelled up the Hollyford in the tracks of Caples and Alabaster. Finally he crossed to the Greenstone, the Mararora and the Von. Miners welcomed him at Queenstown and Hector gracefully gave credit to his predecessors such as Caples and stated that he had had no previous knowledge of them.

His map in the National Archives is a fine piece of work and shows his bestowal of the name of Tutoko to one of the finest mountains in New Zealand. Like McKerrow, Hector had a distinguished career and gained a knighthood and a name as scientist.

The last event, and not the least significant, in 1863 in Otago exploration, was the beginning of exploration by Alphonse J. Barrington. He left Queenstown in November, and after preliminary feints in the Dart valley, returned to the head of Lake Wakatipu. With Edward Dunmore and William Bayliss he tried the Routeburn. His journal for Christmas Day read "had a plum duff boiling; tapped a brandy bottle which we had brought for the occasion, made tea, cooked four Maori hens and spent a jolly afternoon", somewhat of a contrast to the hunger that inevitably lay in the ranges ahead. Two days later, they were joined by "... a man called McGuirk, alias the 'Maori Hen' . . . he has been shepherded by a dozen men on several occasions."

On 30 December they crossed North Col, already known to Cameron and Caples. They went down a pass into Hidden Falls Creek "down precipices fearful to contemplate". Thence they went over Cow Saddle to the head of the Olivine river, where they climbed over a range and descended through wet bush to Lake Alabaster, where they caught twelve pounds of eels. They walked to the outlet of the lake but could not cross the Pyke river. With no tools but a tomahawk they fashioned a boat.

January 1864 began with Dunmore and McGuirk crossing in the boat, while Barrington and Bayliss returned to Wakatipu for provisions. On Barrington's return, James Farrell took the place of Bayliss. At Lake Alabaster they found Dunmore was "a complete living skeleton" and McGuirk had wandered off, never to be seen again. Once again the indefatigable Barrington returned to Wakatipu over the mountains for more stores, and was joined by Antoine Simonin.

Then the three advanced into more new country, a land of rainforests, gorges, flats of unexpected beauty, and always the brooding and glaciated peaks

Icebergs now float in Lake Bonar, where once there was a heavily crevassed glacier to be crossed by Hector and his party.

on the skyline swept by storms from the parent Tasman. The route lay up the Pyke past Lake Wilmot, where there is today a tourist tramping camp. Thence a pass into the Gorge River, a saddle into the Cascade River, and a hazardous trip to the Red Hills district, a place of rare beauty, rare birds and rare minerals, with red rata trailing off into the sombre green of forest. On 4 May Barrington lost his mates in a mist, and suffered ten days of rain and snow, hunger and cold. He wrote "found a root of spear grass, ate some of it, but could not enjoy it raw". Another vivid entry read: "There was nothing for it but desert my swag or die here. . . I threw away everything but my blankets, gun, and a little powder and shot, which was my only dependence." Fortunately the storm lifted and he found his party.

Bad weather returned, and in spite of it the men travelled up the Red Pyke river to a glacier. The entry of 17 May described "a fearful hard day's toil" and referred to a mile long of pure ice, a mountain slope frozen at 75 degrees, and snowberries: "What a sight then met our eyes! Nothing but mountains of snow as far as we could see, in every direction but west." They had reached the Olivine Ice Plateau by a route that is still debated among mountaineers: some favour Demon Gap; others the top of Mt Ellespie. They gained or slipped into the head of the Barrier river, where the deep gorges made progress exhausting for frostbitten men. Back at Lake Alabaster they lived off fern-root (shades of Thomas Brunner). They feasted on a rat the dog had killed in the night, and ate him in three parts as "the sweetest meat we ever ate."

In June the explorers crossed to the head of the Olivine, and later, the Hidden Falls valley "so tired we would give all the world" to be over the Divide.

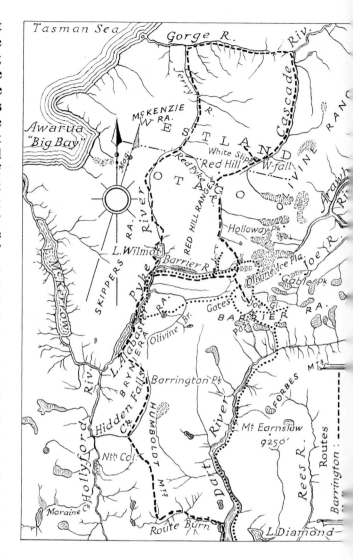

The Olivine Ice Plateau discovered by exploring prospectors in 1864.

The *Dunedin Punch* cartoon of 1865 about Pyke's second crossing of the Haast Pass.

They made the crossing under new snow and on 10 June recorded that all their fasting and praying had entitled them to be saints. Two days later they reached civilisation, where they went to hospital to recover from their privations. Newspapers made much of their work, but only for a time. Friendly miners gave them £40 and a public meeting of thanks, but the new goldfields in Westland put their exploits in the shade, and later into oblivion, till they were rescued by mountaineers such as J. T. Holloway and historians such as W. G. McClymont and Nancy Taylor.

Barrington's trips were in the same superb category as Brunner's great journey and Charles Douglas's many journeys. They are the three great men of New Zealand exploration for the South Island. The enterprise of Jack Holloway added lustre to his alpine re-exploration in the 1930s as well as intelligible interpretation of the Barrington party routes. The Olivine country attracted successors to Barrington and Holloway: Ian Whitehead and parties, Colin Todd, Jim McMahon, Arnold Heinne, John Rundle. Stan Conway and party took me on a marathon trail from the Matukituki to Jackson Bay in 1953 in which the Dart Divide, the Arawhata river, the Olivine Ice Plateau, Mt Holloway, the Red Pyke, Simonin Pass, the Red Hills, and the Cascade valleys were key links topographically as well as mystically with Barrington and Douglas.

This country should be protected as a wilderness area in a national park, but the valuable nickel and other minerals in the Red Hills may make it vulnerable to all the evils of progress. Young New Zealanders for many generations should have testing-grounds like this; where natural boulders can give shelter and huts, tracks and airstrips could be barred. The broken glaciers and unpredictable weather would add to the hazards for travellers; the young generations could feel that they had some of the skills of survival that faced the goldminers of the 1860s.

It is one of the ironies of fame that no worthy mountain features have Barrington's name, yet lesser mortals have won the spurious immortality of such recognition.

Vincent Pyke, Secretary of the Otago goldfields, made the second complete crossing of the Haast Pass to the West Coast. A cartoon shows a moa peering through the scrub at the rather bedraggled efforts of the re-explorers. The Arrow goldfields came into prominence in Otago and one can be sure that the miners covered every nook and cranny of the Shotover. Wood engravings from the *Illustrated London News* and other papers are indeed relevant.

Fiordland was the scene of some arduous work in the decades that followed. There the mountains hemmed in narrow sounds by their precipices. The deeds of the men who came to terms with savage nature reflected the difficulties as surely as the perception of artists such as John Buchanan in the 1860s or John Gully in the 1870s.

Milford Sound, as painted by John Buchanan in the 1860s. Mitre Peak and The Lion are prominent in this panorama from Freshwater Cove.

Mitre Peak and Sinbad Gully are above Milford Sound. This aerial view shows the Bowen Falls (*right centre*) and Freshwater Cove. Mt. Earnshaw is on the horizon (*left distance*).

In 1877 Donald Sutherland made his first visit to Milford Sound. His calibre was shown by his arrival in an open sailing boat in which he was captain, mate and cook, with a dog and livestock as passengers. Three years later he settled at Milford, where his feats became a legend, and the graves of him and his wife may be seen to this day. His memory is safe in the magnificent falls which bear his name; their three leaps total 1,904 feet, a height appropriate to the honour of such an Olympian. What a man! He was a stowaway at the age of twelve, joined the army at sixteen and fought under Garibaldi, became a sailor, sought gold at Gabriels Gully in 1861, fought in the Maori wars, went sealing in Westland, and sailed between Greymouth and Dunedin. He was a hermit to begin with at Milford, but his visitors' book from 1882 shows a regular succession of callers. He took a proprietary pride in Milford Sound and, because Mitre Peak was too tough for him, tried to deny credit to J. R. Dennistoun for being the first to climb it in 1911.

In the early 1880s John Hay crossed Lake Hauroto in a canvas boat and sighted Dusky Sound though he did not reach it. In 1884 Andreas Reischek spent

The picturesque Donald Sutherland.

Quinton McKinnon

Sir Thomas Mackenzie

some time in Dusky Sound where his interests in birds took him into remote places. Sir James Hector gave Reischek a testimonial that he had "undergone very severe personal hardships in his endeavour to solve some of the most difficult problems respecting the habits of our rarest birds". Reischek had been with Haast in the Rakaia in 1878. He was trouble prone, quite apart from providing meals for the sand-flies, which is the right of every traveller to the fiords. He cut his knee badly with an axe; a tree fell on his hut; he nearly perished in a snowstorm on the tops; rats tried to gnaw his beard. He described Dusky as "The dark blue network of water which is the Sound, is sprinkled with wood-decked islands. The coast-line, rimmed with dark rocks, towers almost straight up out of the water, which goes down to a depth of some 900 feet."

Quinton McKinnon and George Tucker were said to have been the first men to climb overland from Lake Te Anau to Caswell Sound in 1877. McKinnon was a great man of Milford exploration and found the pass that bears his name and that in 1888 became the key to the now famous walk from Te Anau to Milford Sound. Another man who endured the difficulties in Fiordland gladly was W. H. Homer, who in 1889 reported to the Chairman of the Lake (Waka-tipu) County Council that he and G. Barber had found a new pass to Milford from the Upper Holly-ford River. Homer held that his Homer Saddle could be pierced by a tunnel — a prophecy that has happily come true for those who drive through to Milford Sound today.

Richard Henry was another man of Fiordland. He explored George Sound with Robert Murrell, a fine pioneer from Lake Manapouri. Public interest was heightened when Professor Mainwaring Brown found a pass from the Spey river, West Arm of Manapouri, that promised to lead to a depot previously estab-lished in Deep Cove, Smith Sound. The Professor vanished in a walk of no great distance from the tent in the Spey Watershed but his body was never found. Murrell, McKinnon, and Thomas Mackenzie, a mem-ber of the House of Representatives, all helped in the searches. This combination of rescue and discovery as motives of exploration was an unusual one.

Mackenzie continued his activity and in 1894 he was with a party that included Murrell. They noted three good saddles and must have descended to the Seaforth valley beyond the Divide, because in a full report presented to Parliament, Mackenzie wrote: "At Loch Maree we had connected with the most north-westerly explorations and observations of Mr District Surveyor Hay." Loch Maree was half way down the Seaforth valley to Dusky Sound. Two years later Mackenzie led an expedition from the

137

Lake Manapouri from the air.
An era has ended: exploration has become exploitation.

A. Talbot (*seated*) and W. G. Grave in the Fiordland bush.

Dusky side but faulty compass work confused him into a wrong identification of the Seaforth river. It was thought essential to prove the existence of a good tourist route from Manapouri to Dusky. The previous uncertainties were skilfully explained after a magnificent trip made in 1897 by the surveyor E. H. Wilmot, who linked the Spey on the Manapouri side with the Seaforth to Dusky Sound, and recommended that at the best the passes were only suitable for foot tracks. He also found and used Wilmot Pass to Doubtful Sound.

Richard Henry spent some years in the period 1894-1904 in Dusky Sound and though limited by the broken country made many inland trips and added much new information.

The practical result of the combined work of Mackenzie and Wilmot was that overland trails of great interest were opened up. Robert Murrell maintained a great interest in his backblocks, and his sons also made notable explorations. Leslie Murrell was a guide and hunter of great renown in the wapiti country of Fiordland, and his enterprise perfected many of the tracks in use today. J. R. Murrell explored with Edgar R. Williams in the Milford country before the first world war. Norman Murrell, another guide and a man of the high snows as much as of the bush, added lustre to the family.

Wilmot's work has been recorded for all time by

the use of his name on the pass that carries the road from the West Arm of Manapouri to the sea at Deep Cove and thus serves the huge Manapouri power project as well as tourists. The last sixty years have seen some continued exploration, so well are the fastnesses of Fiordland defended by the weather and climate.

One of the most exciting finds in the Milford region was in 1909, when W. G. Grave and A. Talbot opened up a new high-level pass to the Sound from the Hollyford, the result of persistent enterprise and some useful intuition. Grave's daughter published a record of his bush-whacking and mountaineering that added up to genuine exploration. Grave characterised the difficulties as vertical mountain walls and an annual rainfall of some 200 inches a year: nearly seventeen feet of rain a year is an awful lot of water. In the summer it rains about five days in the week. That is bad enough on a well-bridged motor route but it is intimidating when pushing on foot through the thickest of undergrowth, up mossy cliffs, and across rivers of great treachery.

Grave's 1897 expedition was inspired by a report that the virgin Mt Tutoko, rising some 9,000 feet above sea level, was of volcanic origin. This surmise proved false but, although Grave could not scale the peak, his trip up the Tutoko branch of the Cleddau started his good career with the solid achievement of sterling attempt. He gained some experience in the discovery of overland routes from Te Anau to Bligh and Sutherland Sounds, through the inevitable gorges, torrents and jungle, and with companions of high intellectual attainment: Sir Thomas Hunter of Victoria University, and the astronomer Gifford. By 1907 Grave was determined to try every branch of the Cleddau for the pass he felt must exist. One branch, the Donne, proved hopeless. Another, the Gulliver, was as bad, and its tributary no better; cliffs always barred the way.

Back in civilisation, Grave studied his photographs and realised that there was a possibility he hopefully called the Esperance. He determined to try from the Hollyford side. Investigation of the moraine branch of the Hollyford gave exacting climbing but no positive results for a pass. The next year, 1909, the Marian branch provided the same tough fare. Early in 1910 Grave and Talbot tried to force a crossing of Homers Saddle, but three hours' work could only take them 150 feet on the Milford side. Wisely Grave looked for another route. They climbed a steep rock and snow peak of 6,000 feet and later returned to the camp. The following day they pursued their advantage from the crest of Homers Saddle and over the peak of Mt Macpherson till they could traverse a ridge towards grassy bluffs and rock ledges to the Esperance valley below.

By 8 p.m. they had to rope down an unexpected precipice. Let Grave convey his own sense of drama: "We had now cut off all chance of climbing back. Downward we must go. Each further stage was accomplished by tying the ends of a piece of snowgrass with a piece of string, and passing the rope through. There was not much danger of the snowgrass giving way. The chief risk was that the string might slip off the grass. When our supply of string gave out, we used pieces of our bootlaces. Talbot, being a much better climber than I, had the more difficult and dangerous work of coming last."

What a descent! Their daring was justified. At 9 p.m. they reached the safety of scrub slopes. They had a cold night with a wet fog as a blanket. The next morning they saw that by match-light on the previous night they had ventured in a search for water on a bluff sheer for 400 feet. When the fog cleared, they got down to the valley floor and so to Milford. Not content with the discovery of their pass, they returned eleven months later and from the Milford side made variations in their initial route that eliminated two of the most hazardous sections. Grave summed up his exploration by writing: "The track across the mountain will never be as easy as that over McKinnon Pass, which I have known ladies to cross in evening shoes. It will be more after the nature of the Copland Pass at Mt Cook." Grave, the solicitor

and mountaineer explorer, died in 1935, and his biographer in the New Zealand Alpine Club *Journal* quoted aptly from the *Odes* of Horace a translation: "I have erected a monument more lasting than brass."

Although some mountain climbers are simply peak-baggers for names or records, there have been others who have used their mountaineering experience to give them information to solve or help others to solve topographical puzzles. Thus the work of the alpine topographers has helped exploration and at times has itself been exploration. Edgar R. Williams was a man who specialised in alpine exploration in the Fiordland region for a period of fifty-five years. Others in this field have included Kurt Suter of Switzerland, Marie Byles of Australia, Paul Powell, Jack Ede, and Doctors Roland Rodda and Lindsay Stewart. They have made it possible for the *avant grade* such as the ranger Harold Jacobs to do new routes up mountains.

One of the most striking lessons both from the Milford explorations and climbs was that those who made them had to combine the qualities of bushman and mountaineer. The ability to remain in good humour when food was short, rivers high, and barometer low, was another necessary virtue. It has been in these combinations of skills that the New Zealand mountain flavour has been apparent: compass work, cooking, resource, endurance and the ability to admit defeat. These essentials were as inherent as the capacity to use rope and ice-axe, slasher and camera. That Grave and the other explorers could accomplish so much in limited holidays and in limited periods of fine weather has underlined the attractions of the challenge bravely accepted.

At the end of the first world war the Fowler brothers and G. Jacquiery made several explorations west of Manapouri. Other forms of pioneering have made headlines, such as the re-discovery by Dr G. B. Orbell in 1948 of the once extinct Takahe.

Other events of importance to the natural and physical sciences have some place in exploration of country. The New Zealand and American Fiordland Expedition of 1949 in the Caswell and George Sound watershed took many specialists to new fields in appalling weather. The data compiled by A. L. Poole covered research on the deer population, the geology, vegetation, fauna, fish and birds in the tradition of Captain Cook's scientists. A young and energetic survey party accomplished valuable topographical results. The leader wrote: "There seems to be no escape from strenuous work if the mapping of further areas of Fiordland is undertaken." Thus the fieldwork of today is related to pioneer discoveries by the common factor of sweat and swags, patience and initiative.

The academics also have helped on the frontiers of contemporary exploration. In 1953 a seven-man party from the Canterbury Museum explored part of the Murchison Range at the head of the South Fiord of Lake Te Anau. They mapped a considerable area and made the first ascent of lonely Mount Irene, one of the most inaccessible and weatherbound peaks of a soggy region.

There are great advantages today in the aid given by amphibian aircraft and helicopters to deer and wapiti hunters and tourists in Fiordland. They can get provisions at the flash of a radio signal. Nevertheless the deerhunters deserve a special page in exploration. They take their place as the 1970 version of the 1863 goldminer: inarticulate unless loosened up by a bit of grog; wide roving and incredibly fit; generally unable to write reports or to remember topographical details; living for the discoveries of the moment; accomplishing much travel in hitherto unvisited places.

There has been a great improvement in maps to the point of a revolution. When I first went into the mountains in 1929 as a young man with ambitions to be an explorer of sorts one of my tasks was to help my friends get compass bearings. A new map was being made by the Survey Department, and the work done even by amateurs was not to be sneezed at. So far from being ignored we were lent instruments, just as Douglas was lent a compass and given field books. A winter climb of Avalanche Peak above Arthur's Pass was for me a matter of taking a full circle of bearings to all known points and calling them out to my companion with a notebook. One and all got frozen hands.

The Southern Alps maps for the regions between the Waimakariri and the Rangitata were largely maps showing the boundaries of sheep runs, but the errors in rivers and locations of peaks were surprising. The Westland maps were better because Mueller, Roberts and Douglas had been so careful with detail, and their successors, the geological surveyors, had a vested interest in accuracy. But it was still necessary for my generation to keep an eye open for errors.

Today the situation is different. The completion of aerial mapping; the use of photogrammetry; the production of detailed maps with contours to every feet and the topography to a scale of one inch to a mile: these things have shrunk the remaining exploration to minor dimensions. Now if a party wants to go where the foot of man has never trod its members fly into the foot of a face and with superb technique force their way up, overhangs and all, by the latest engineering equipment, knowing that if they come to grief they may be rescued by a helicopter patrol.

Epilogue: A Personal Note

At the risk of being asked for details, I here maintain that I do know of some remaining uncrossed cols, unclimbed ridges, even virgin peaks, but the exploration inherent in the examination of these features is shadowy compared with the substance of my joy when as a young climber I could tramp up some valleys knowing that no one knew exactly what was on the other side. Under the circumstances I record my admiration of the face climbers[1] and rejoice that the Caroline face of Mt Cook was in 1970 twice ascended without accident. At the same time, and as a veteran, I do not envy anyone when I remember the opportunities for minor but practical exploration that came my way at intervals. Similarly I could count as friend, as well as venerated acquaintance or boss, such men as Sir Arthur Dudley Dobson, Sir George Harper, Arthur P. Harper, the Graham brothers as guides, Jack Clarke, Edgar R. Williams, Jack Holloway, and the daughters of J. H. Baker and Gerhard Mueller.

Enough of name-dropping. Let me now admit that I never met the men in whom I was also interested: among them, Barrington, Lauper, Brunner, Douglas, Arawata Bill. Yet I found my affinity in other ways. When editing Brunner, and years later, Douglas, I dreamt (literally) that I was on expeditions with them, in the same mystical way in which Dr J. C. Beaglehole could talk to Captain Cook's men at dawn on the beach of Mercury Bay when he was pondering the events of 1769. I can still recall the sweetness of the flute played by Sir Arthur Dudley Dobson and the strength of the billy tea given to me by Jack Clarke when I called at his roadman's camp.

So I shall finish this narrative, as I began it, with the claim that I have dreamt of some of the experiences the explorers themselves have described. This is both an identification of myself with some of the explorers and a justification for my existence; and, for having as a family man taken some physical risks in following some of their trails. In travelling in sometimes dangerous and difficult terrain I have conquered my own weakness and my fear of the unknown. The succour of my predecessors and their spirit, have lived on in the alpine and forest wilderness. May future generations of New Zealanders find for themselves the inspiration of the explorers.

John Dobrée Pascoe,

289 Muritai Road,
Eastbourne, Wellington,
New Zealand, 1971.

[1] I am proud that my nephew Dr Jonathan Pascoe is a member of the face and rescue team, the *elite* of mountaineers.

Index

Numerals in bold type refer to illustrations; "plate" refers to colour illustrations.

SAINT LOUIS ART MUSEUM LIBRARY